MW00416252

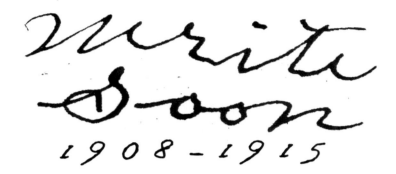

Write Soon
1908-1915

FIRST HAND HISTORY
through the
CORRESPONDENCE OF A
SOUTHERN VIRGINIA FAMILY

BY KYLE GRIFFITH

To Melvin — I hope this book can bring
you great memories and that you appreciate
our Board family's mention.

[signature]

DRY FORK

2019

THIS BOOK IS DEDICATED TO:

My mother, *Lisa Powell*
My grandmother, *Margaret Grant Gupton*
My great-aunt, *Ruby Grant Hardin*
My great-aunt, *Hazel Grant Morris*
My great-uncle, *Herman Grant*
My cousin, *Mittie Lou Edmunds*
All of my cousins who share the Pruett family
& all of my future descendants

Cover artwork, all inside designs, writing, and
transcriptions by Kyle Griffith.

WHY I WROTE THIS
And Why it Applies to You

These cards hold jubilation, despair, tribulation, anticipation, satire, togetherness, and quite surely every step in between. I like to think that this collection of letters is not simply an archive of my family's history, but a representation of most every rural family in the southern United States. These letters tell a story. It is my story, but it is also yours. This is the collective story of our heritage; my family just happens to be the characters, though their actions hit home with you just as much as they do me.

I hope that this book can serve as a safe house for the memories that are slipping away from modern life. Sure, there are plenty of people alive in 2019 who are lucky enough to have known family and friends born in the 1860's, '70's, and '80's; though, they exist now only as memories. Unfortunately, those memories are not always shared. *Most* fortunately, some of the memories were written down and photographed just as they happened. It would be selfish of me to withhold this treasure which I have been blessed with, for it can stand to reimburse those whose arms lay barren from heirlooms.

In January and February of 2019, I put together an extensive PowerPoint presentation on a select few of these letters. I presented it first at the Danville Museum of Fine Arts & History in Danville, Virginia. I expected twenty to twenty-five people to show up, but over fifty viewers crammed into the UDC room, some without chairs, to listen to me spout my findings.

My wonderful cousin, Mittie Lou Edmunds, has given me the majority of the letters featured in this book. She is the daughter of Nina Pruett, mentioned prevalently throughout the book. Mittie's grandmother, Mittie Watson Pruett, is also a star in this book as will become evident.

Without the collective efforts of my relatives to protect these letters, photos, and items enough to reach the present day where they may be preserved permanently, this book would not exist, and my life would be empty of its passion for this elaborate history. No degree of gratitude could ever convey the extent I am beholden.

TABLE OF CONTENTS

INTRODUCTION

Who was Granny Meadows? Here I am, under no voluntary decision, placed in this house of maternal patriarchy—every family member bearing a different surname—yet another is brought to my attention? Quaint names with hollow meaning often skipped in and out of our dinner parley. To the older members of the family, the names were a gift of insight, esteem, sentiment—names, which bore no perfect portrayal of the true human form through simple verbal depiction, unacquainted with my life. To my family, they are the names of their past; though, to me, they are the names of my future.

Once I was old enough to find interest in the past, I learned that my house—my very room—was the lodging of my great-great-grandmother, Permelia Alice Pruett Meadows, born in 1881. I heard she was a stern and small-framed woman with snowy hair always lighter than the nearest white object cited for comparison, just like my grandmother. I was told she slept on an itchy straw tick bed with a feather-stuffed pillow just across from where I have slept all my life. 'Granny Meadows' became not simply a term, but clues for an idea submerged in imagination. I pictured her sleeping in her primitive bed, sauntering through the house as one does in advanced age, planting flowers in the garden, watering her plants. She filled my imagination; though, I did not know the face which bore her name.

As time passed, I gradually found more photographs of those deceased family members I had heard so much about. I saw my great-grandparents for the first time; I saw their brothers, their sisters, and eventually, I saw Alice. This remainder of her likeness was stashed in a drawer in my grandmother's living room—I pulled out the tattered brown photo of a woman standing in her grassless yard aptly wearing a long-sleeved floral dress with a tidy, white full body apron. She was accented by a head of pure white feathery hair, just like my grandmother.

Later, almost as a prophetic incentive to make genealogy my passion, I was given a collection of priceless heirlooms which once belonged to Alice: a pair of her glasses, her notebook, her stove-top coffee maker, so on; it seemed endless. Upstairs in my own house sat an old-fashioned chest which I had only just discovered when searching that day. It contained Alice's hat and two pairs of

Write Soon | Kyle Griffith

her shoes—one for daily wear, one for Sunday's best. With these additions, Alice evolved past the status of an imaginary impression or term; she became a true being, yet long gone from this world, but having left her undying mark on my maternal heritage and my sacred Dry Fork house on this Pittsylvania County hill engulfed by *Virginia, the delightful.*

One afternoon, I received a noticeably thick letter in the mail from my grandmother's cousin, Mittie. I often wrote letters to her discussing the family history. In the envelope were vibrant, ornate postcards of considerable age covered with writing—extremely cursive, almost indecipherable lettering which I was taken aback by at my first glance. The writing held the unmistakable curling and angular quality only produced by the hands of those over one hundred years ago in a way seemingly never replicated perfectly today. I found the letters to be by those named 'Ida,' 'Willie,' 'Nina,' 'Grandmother,' and—"Alice."

Alice had come to life—I lived in her room, I knew her name, I saw her face, I held her belongings, I touched her clothing, and I heard her words. In a sense, I am her, in that I continue her bloodline, and that she is my maternal lineage. The chance that I may be well acquainted with someone born so far in the past is one of the greatest gifts I can bare.

How could this honor be enhanced? The answer is 'Grandmother.' Not my grandmother, not even my grandmother's grandmother, but a generation preceding that. Delaware Green Watson Pruett, the one who began it all. My x3 great-grandmother, Delaware, was born in 1841. I got to know her simply as 'Grandmother,' and she opened the past up to me as if it were yesterday's news through her letters. This publication exhibits her and her children's letters from 1908-1915.

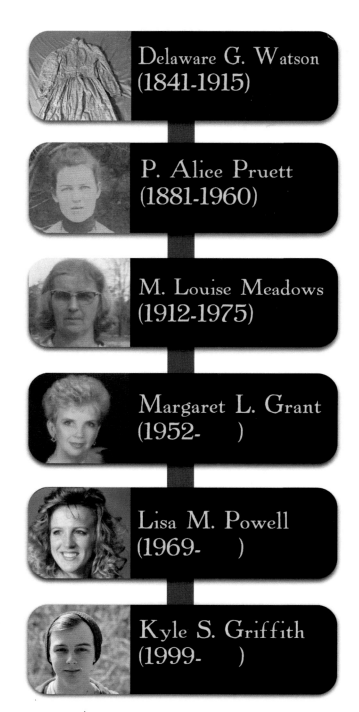

Delaware G. Watson
(1841-1915)

P. Alice Pruett
(1881-1960)

M. Louise Meadows
(1912-1975)

Margaret L. Grant
(1952-   )

Lisa M. Powell
(1969-   )

Kyle S. Griffith
(1999-   )

SEVEN GENERATIONS IN DRY FORK

M iss Delaware Watson directed her horse-drawn buggy south west in a hurry, for her man was coming home to-day. It was February 1865 as Dellie parted from her congregation of Watson cousins who took residence in Chatham, Virginia. The War Between the States was on its last leg, but Ephraim had been mustered out and was headed home (He served as a Private in the 38th VA Infantry, Company D and fought in the Battle of Gettysburg). Dellie traveled to Dry Fork, Virginia—a proud and thriving community overlooked by the old White Oak Mountain. She met with Ephraim and the two married that November. They moved out to Callands, Virginia where they began a homestead and had ten children; only one of which—Charles—did not live to adulthood (or so that is how I surmise it all to have happened).

Neither Ephraim nor Delaware believed in photography, so neither ever had their pictures made. Photography was widely thought to be a sinful practice capable of imprisoning one's soul for eternity. Alternatively, all nine of their children had their photos taken.

Around 1890, the two bought a house on present day Irish Road diagonal from where Dame Memorial Church is was. At that time, the area was known as Weal, Virginia (a sub-community of Dry Fork) and it was near the Lewis Cassidy ("L. C.") Giles store, which also served as the post office. Ephraim owned a twenty-acre triangular portion of property where he farmed tobacco and partnered with his childhood neighbor, Hezekiah Ford Pigg, who ran Pigg's Mill. His daughter-in-law Rada Pigg was the postmistress in Dry Fork. Ephraim passed away while working in the yard in February 1907 and was found by his wife, Delaware.

Hezekiah Ford Pigg
(1823-1908)

Their daughter, Permelia Alice Pruett, was named for Delaware's mother, Permelia Giles; though, she was simply called Alice. Alice married a farmer from Callands named Dock Franklin Meadows in 1901 and they stayed next to Ephraim and Delaware.   Around 1911, Dock and Alice moved out to be farmhands until they could afford another house by working on the land of Mr. Edgar Green. Alice kept her mother updated on the state of their health and work for a few years through the exchange of post cards; though, Delaware's health was declining, and she eventually passed away in December 1915. Eventually, Dock and Alice bought some of Mr. Green's land and lived in a small, two building log home with a runway down the middle. Each building had two rooms; the left building was used as the kitchen, but all four rooms were used for sleeping. Dock and Alice had seven children together. The ceilings in their home were about six feet tall, and all four of their sons eventually grew to be taller than six feet. Dock worked as a farmer and a gravedigger. Quoting S. Dail Yeatts' book *Along the Dry Fork Road*, "[Dock] was employed by many families to dig the grave of a loved one. He was considered the best grave engineer in the community."

Edgar Green
(1873-1950)

Around 1930, the Meadows family got new neighbors: the Grant family from up the road. John Thomas Grant moved into a house beside Dock and Alice with his wife Mary and seven children. They were the cousins to Charlie Washington Grant who ran the celebrated Grant's Grocery up the road a few years later.

George W. Grant
(1912-1969)

John had a son named George W. Grant who began to work as a farmhand for Dock. George never knew what the 'W' stood for in his middle name, but he believed it was Wilford, although it has been written down as Wilbur, Wilburn, and even Washington. He often worked all day in the yard and stayed the night in the barn. One of Alice's daughters, Louise, found a liking to George Grant and decided that if she married him, then her parents would let him stay in the house—and they did. He and Louise were born only ten days apart in 1912. In 1933, they were married in the parsonage to the Dry Fork Emmanuel Pentecostal Holiness Church; About ten years later, the parsonage was put up for sale. It was just down the road from their house, and it was delightfully sentimental in value, so they bought it.

Dock came down with Tuberculosis, which paired with congestive heart failure in leading to his death in 1942, just shy of his 60th birthday. On his death certificate, he is also noted as having chronic nephritis (lung inflammation) and osteosclerosis (abnormal bone hardening). His son Harry Meadows remembered Dock staying in a shed in order to keep his children from becoming sick. Harry took plates of food out to him daily, sat them outside of the door, and knocked so his father could eat.

Dock F. Meadows
(1882-1942)

While Alice was increasing in age daily, her home was no longer suitable for her, especially without Dock by her side. There was no running water, so it was an ordeal to trek down the hill for water and back up with a heavy bucket, and her children were old enough to move out and marry. Her sons made a pact that they would all get together and build their mother a house if some of the children agreed to care of her. Oscar, Joe, Otha, and Harry collected what materials they could using wartime rations and built a house next to Louise and her husband George Grant in the parsonage. The house was erected using no firm measurements—five rooms downstairs, three rooms upstairs—the biggest room being the kitchen, for the family enjoyed their home cooking. There was no bathroom added and only enough electricity for lights and a few radios. There was no television, no telephones, no electric stoves, no air conditioning, but there was a freezer. Most rooms had a wood stove for heating. Alice took the first room to the left, and her children Oscar, Nettie, and Harry agreed to live with her. Another child, Cassie, lived just across the street next to Joe Lynch's blacksmith shop. (Joe Lynch's wife was Ruth Pruett, the sister to Alice).

George Grant, my great-grandfather, worked as a farmhand in the morning and worked at the renowned Dan River Textile Mill in the afternoon as a cloth dyer. With Louise, he had six children: Ruby Alice, Posey Anderson, Hazel Mae, Fred Thomas, Margaret Louise, and George Herman Grant. Louise made clothing and quilts and sold them for profit. Other than that, she worked in the yard keeping up the garden and flowers most of the day. Oscar Meadows also took a job in the Mill, which is where he met his soon-to-be wife Reggie "Elva" Evalyn Meadors (no relation). Harry eventually moved away and Oscar brought his newlywed wife into the house. She was a city girl from Danville—she and Nettie did not

Oscar F. Meadows
(1908-1986)

get along at all. Elva insisted on bringing her electronics and other modern belongings into the house, whereas the Meadows family were old fashioned and intended to stay that way; Nettie did not allow it. God forbid if Elva brought outside food, especially "them old hot dogs" that were a disgrace to the health. Alice grew turnips beside the house, as well as corn, potatoes, and a few other foods. Margaret remembers her grandmother Alice feeding her slices of turnips when she visited her as a child, just as she did years later when she became my grandmother. Alice slept on an old bed with a straw-filled mattress, even into the age where such a mattress was obsolete; she did so out of preference (I reckon it's comfortable to some people). Oscar eventually left his job at the mill and began his own business: Meadows Grocery. The building operated in a few locations until it replaced the former V. T. Crane's store in Dry Fork.

All the family were punctual and dedicated members of the Emmanuel Pentecostal Holiness Church, and they had been for decades. Margaret had perfect attendance for 11 years without missing a Sunday. George even helped with the additions on the church in 1955. The teachings of the church helped to shape the reserved and old-fashioned mannerisms of the family since it was part of the practice to refrain from owning a television, playing cards, dancing, or for women to wear pants—only dress skirts. The family were already old-fashioned, which is one reason why the church meant so much to them all.

In 1960, Alice's health began to degenerate. It is said that she asked her son Harry to get her a cup of strawberry ice cream from Oscar's store, but she passed away by the time he returned with it; she was 78 years old. It was June 10, 1960—nineteen days before her birthday—from congestive heart failure. Nettie, Oscar, and his wife Elva continued to live in the house.

My grandmother, Margaret Grant, married in 1967 to Jerry Powell. Less than a year later, they had a daughter, Robin Powell. In 1969, another was on the way, and Margaret's father George Grant was declining in health due to cancer. He was admitted to Danville Memorial Hospital and passed away on January 21, 1969. Seven months later, my mother, Lisa Powell, was born.

Louise passed away a few years later in 1975 from colon cancer. Shortly after, the parsonage house burned down. While it was a tragedy, there were a few pieces of furniture and items saved. The rest of the house was bulldozed and a new brick home was erected several yards from the previous home, so Robin and Lisa were able to grow up beside their great-grandmother's home where Nettie, Oscar, and Elva still lived.

Nettie cooked breakfast for her brother starting at 5 AM on the wood stove; he ate and then he headed to his store. She also cooked lunch for when he returned on his break. Then, she cooked dinner for everyone at 5 PM. The ceiling is still charcoal grey from the constant smoke of the wood stove. To bathe, everyone hauled a tub full of heated well water up the steep, steep steps to wash off using a cloth. There was one electrical socket per room, usually used for a radio. There was no television or telephone; Nettie and Oscar read the Bible for fun. Oscar recorded the number of times that he finished reading it in its entirety followed by the date.

Nettie G. Meadows
(1903-1997)

In the middle of the night in 1986, Oscar got up to use the bathroom; it was just after 12. There was no bathroom in the house, but they had an outhouse and used chamber pots. While using the chamber pot, he simply fell back on to the bed—and that was the end of his life. It was his 77th birthday. He had been declining in health for a few years due to lung cancer.

One day, Elva was carrying a tub of water up the stairs to bathe with, when suddenly, she slipped. There was no hand rail and the steps were so tall that they may as well have been two placed on top of each other. The older someone is, the less they can recover from injuries, and this fall broke both of Elva's arms and her neck. To this day there is a dent in the wall from her head and shoe skid marks on the wall much higher than anyone should be able to reach. Elva didn't die from this fall, but she endured its pain and eventually healed about as well as one could hope to. The jar to her head influenced the arrival of Alzheimer's Disease. Eventually, the illness took her over. Both Nettie and Elva passed away in 1997. Elva was placed in a nursing home when she could no longer be adequately cared for and Nettie lived the last few years with her niece.

My mother, Lisa Powell, moved into the house in the mid 1990's. At that point, for the first time in the house's fifty-year lifespan, a bathroom was finally added. She claimed the room which belonged to Oscar and Elva. Nettie's room was made into a storage room; although, in 1999, that was quick to change.

My mother was told she would never be able to have children by multiple sources, but after five positive pregnancy tests, she decided she was pregnant. The room was swiftly made into a room for me. By that late November, I occupied the very room that once belonged to my great-great grandmother, Alice. In fact, almost twenty years later, it is the room I sit in while I type these very words.

Louise Meadows Grant at the house in 1949 and again in 2016

Alice Pruett Meadows on the front porch ca. 1955 and again in 2017
*note the same metal chair is visible
*the large plant draped over the porch is morning glories

Mary
Ida
Pruett
(1886–1980)

HALL OF FAME
Meet the Pruett Family

Each member of the Pruett family held his or her own unique and defining qualities—surely applicable candidates for portraying most any Southern family of the time period. **Ida** was a small-framed, humorous, hug-and-kiss type with a love for her family. She loved to laugh and wrote the most out of the rest of her siblings. Although she married twice, she never had children of her own and lived a long life. **Willie** was mostly business and did not engage in much small talk. While he was not the best at spelling, he enjoyed numbers well enough to become vice-president of the Chatham Savings Bank in Chatham, Virginia. Most of his letters proudly state the amount of money he received for the year's tobacco sale. **John** was a family man as well and got along with his brother, Willie. Farming was his passion which he followed his entire life. He made a fine father and grandfather as well, often known to make whistles and toys for his children. **Alice** was a stern woman but still held a soft spot for her family. She loved to garden and was very sentimental. She held on to the olden ways of living for as long as she was able to and raised seven fine children. **Mittie** was constantly involved in the family as well. As the wife of John, she made sure that her children, **Nina** and **Aubrey**, got to see and keep a relationship with their grandmother, **Delaware**, and kept her up to date on their actions. **Joe** did not often write to his siblings, but he lived with Delaware, his mother, and helped her through the death of his father, **Ephraim**. He took care of all the farm work and selling while also keeping a close bond with his mother. **Lillie** was always a beam of sunshine—forever cheerful in her letters and kept a happy marriage. **Sue** loved farming as well and made a good pair with her husband, Willie. She was the sister of Mittie as well, although, Sue did not have children. John, Mittie, Willie, and Sue all bought a house together in Chatham. While this was not the whole of the family, these were the ones who stayed in touch as much as they could. So much, in fact, that they unknowingly provided the very substantial fillings of a book to be made from their daily exchanges.

William
Thomas
Pruett
(1868-1945)

John
Ballard
Pruett
(1873–1960)

Permelia
Alice Pruett
(1881–1960)

Mittie Cora
(Watson)
Pruett
(1875–1946)

Nina E.
Pruett
(1909-2000)

Write Soon | Kyle Griffith

Aubrey J.
Pruett
(1910-1966)

Joseph "Joe" E. Pruett (1883–1916)

Write Soon | Kyle Griffith

Lillie Carr
Pruett
(1889-1957)

Susan H.
Watson
Pruett
(1864–1933)

VERNACULAR
of the Old South

As if it were not enough that the handwriting of the past is nearly indecipherable to many who attempt to read it today, there were many unique expressions and labels that have fallen out from popular use since then. Moreover, spelling was based on the way the words were pronounced, which was oftentimes *incorrectly*—or was it? Many of the phrases have clear origins in languages separate from English or from more archaic forms of English. Overall, the pronunciation of words relies on frequent use of additional or substituted r- sounds in words (i.e. fellow = feller; wash = warsh). This is known as a *rhotic accent*. Another strong trait still alive in some southern communities is the addition of the prefix '*a-*' in front of a verb to provide a better continuation of speech. For example, "I'm agoing to town." There is also reduction, which is the shortening of multiple commonly grouped words into one optimal word, such as '*ain't*.'

am not = amn't = an't = ain't

The seclusion of rural and mountainous Virginia minimized further linguistic advancement from the original colloquialisms learned in Scotland, Ireland, France, and Elizabethan England. The addition of the prefix 'h-' to a word is used for accentuation, just as one stresses the syllable of a word for clarification. For example, one may say '*h*it' in stead of 'it.' In one case, '*h*ain't' is the word 'ain't,' but stressed. Further use of the word 'hain't' or 'han't' shows that it can also be the contraction of 'has not.' Though, the word used as 'haint' (not a contraction, but a noun) is a ghost.

Throughout the couple hundred letters in my possession written by my Pruett family, there is not one single instance of punctuation. There are no periods, no commas, no apostrophes, nothing. The only form of separation between sentences if often the use of the word 'well' just as one would use it to begin or change a topic in conversation.

Word	Usage	Meaning
Toble	Doing just toble	Tolerable
Lones	I am very lones	Lonesome
Moast	Are you moast ready?	Almost
Hant	She hant got better yet	Has not
Gaily	I am gaily today	Well/Happy
Ought to	You ought to come	Should
Dent	I dent see any	Did not
Preaching	I went to preaching	Sunday worship
Curing	Have you cured?	Drying tobacco
Snaps	My snaps is ready	Green beans
Sallet	I have sallet to cook	Turnip greens
Jug fill	Ready to get my jug fill	Alcohol
Mity	I get mity lones	Mighty/Very
Own	Gettin own fine	On/Along
Jubbelee	Have a jubbelee time	Wonderful/Great

Above is a list of a few words and phrases that appear throughout the collection of letters that may be unfamiliar to most readers. Through a mixture of slang and misspellings, many local families developed their own rendition of the English language—I call it *Southside Virginian.*

CHAPTER ONE
The Good Ole Days

Whereas, lying just beneath the surface of modern life and all the situations that arise from it are the past experiences and memories that have brought each and every one to the moment that is *now*. For you, *now* is the time spent reading these words; although, *now* you have already read them. Wasn't that splendid? Yet, while those announcements were not so profound, there is an underlying idea—that, while a chapter of someone's life may not appear so clearly life-changing or enjoyable during the experience itself, once the memory of that experience can be applied in comparison to how much life changed afterward, only then will the chapter reveal itself to have been magical. That is the brilliant nature of the past.

Therefore, in this moment in time where nostalgia and retro-inspirations are at their peak, I call attention to a time which so many refer to as "the good old days." It is 1908 and your lifelong husband has passed away leaving you frail and unable to gather adequate resources to survive. If no seeds have been planted, there is nothing to eat or sell. If wood has not been chopped, there is no heat. If water has not been gathered, there is nothing to drink. The neighbors have lost six children to small pox. The other neighbor has lost two husbands to tuberculosis. You are just happy to be alive, for these moments are blessings and will be remembered as "the good old days."

But, through the tribulations and brotherhood of people surviving together and sharing the little bit that they have amongst themselves is what makes these old days good. Simplicity, determination, strong will, honesty—it can be said that these attributes are losing strength through time. Just as it is common to respect a veteran for the efforts he or she has withstood, it is most certainly decided out of respect rather than envy to take a time known for widespread bother and toil and call it "the good old days."

The Measles is Near
Alice to Delaware

"Jun the 10 Hody mama how are you well I hope I am well as common I was sorry to hear that your cow was dead well we hant got the measles yet they hant got no closer then Richard Goads yet I get Mity lones Dock wont let me go no where and wont let no body come but Rinner and Mr Clarke folks on the count of the measles write soon and come soon from Alice to Mother."

"Richard Goad" refers to Richard Goard who lived down the road and eventually became Alice's neighbor. At the time of this letter, Alice was pregnant with Louise, my great-grandmother, who married George Grant, the grandson of Richard Goard (which makes him my x3 great-grandfather).

John Richard Goard (1861-1932)

Small Pox & Colds
Alice to Delaware

"Well Mamma I will answer your posted I was glad to hear from you I hope this will find you stranger This leaves us all up the children has about got over ther colds Lueasy hant got well but she is better she has got so she can sleep none we had to set up with her every night for over a week we hant got the small pox yet I heard of no body having the small pox but Claud Hardy well you must come soon I will come as soon as I can from Alice to Mamma good by"

Lewis "Claude" Hardy lived down the road from Alice and was not killed by the small pox. He lived until 1948.

"Lueasy" is referring to Alice's daughter "Louise."

Lewis Claude Hardy (1891-1948)

Death and Sickness
Ida to John

"Hello Jack how are you well I hope I am well how are you Getting on farming this fine wether are you done planting corn and how many tobacco hills have you made farm work is going on veary slow up in this part well I have no much to write Charlie Stow died last after noon Mr Scot Watson has bin on the sick list for som time there is right much sickness about now The mumps is among hear I have to keep closs now I have been in one place so long I have wore the hide off in some places Well you must come soon Bring Mittie and the baby child soon by by from M I to John"

Scott Watson was Delaware's brother. He did not die from the mentioned sickness.

George Scott Watson (1859-1922)

Ephraim's Pipe

This small, separable wooden pipe was most likely the posession of Ephraim Pruett, husband of Delaware. This is assumed to be true due to the nature of its finding. The pipe was in a box of Delaware's personal documents and belongings; in with the documents were rolled up and folded receipts for Ephraim's tobacco sales in the early-to-mid 1890's. Notice the signs of usage around the lid.

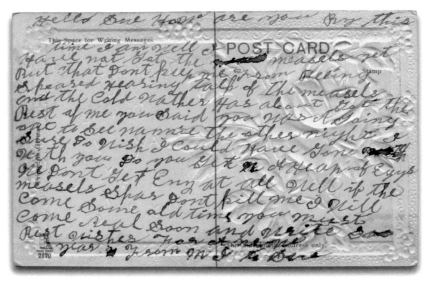

The Measels Spar
Ida to Sue

"Hello Sue how are you by this time I am well I have not got the measels yet but that dont keep me from beeing speared hearing talk of the measels and the cold wather has about got the best of me you said you was a going out to see nannie the other night I sure do wish I could have gone with you do you got a heap of eggs we dont get eny at all well if the measels spar dont kill me I will come some old time you must come real soon and write soon best wishes for a new year from M I to Sue"

By 1912, an average of 6,000 Americans deaths per year were reportedly caused by the measles. By the 1980's, the impact of the measles had declined to affect only 1 in every 100,000 people. The disease was not considered eliminated in the U.S. until the year 2000.

See page **60** for information on *Nannie.*

Scared of Breaking Out
Ida to Willie

"Hello Willie how are you I am scared I bet I get the measels I was with a girl last Sunday and she broke out with the measels Monday night mamma said tell you to come Sunday well I cant write no more now you must all come soon from M I Pruett"

Measles is a highly contagious virus spread through coughing and sneezing. The airspace in which an infected person has coughed or sneezed can stay infected for up to two hours afterward. It takes up to 12 days for any signs of the measles to take effect. Thankfully, Ida did not get the measles.

Looking for Robert to Die
Delaware to Aubrey

"Hello Aubrey how are you well I hope I dont feel well this morning say if you have got large anough to go to town and drive the horse you can come up here and see me I have got two chickens this morning well I have no news to write only they all looking for Robert Giles to die his father is at his bed side come soon and write soon from grandmother"

Robert Hayes Giles was the son of Lewis Cassidy "L.C." Giles, the local postmaster and general store owner in Wilmer (a section of Dry Fork now on Irish Road). The mail arrived at L.C.'s store and the locals came to pick it up from him. His son Robert lived in Lynchburg with his wife, Carrie. Robert contracted Tuberculosis and passed away in 1915 at the age of 37. This would have been big news in the neighborhood since L.C. was gone from the community for a while.

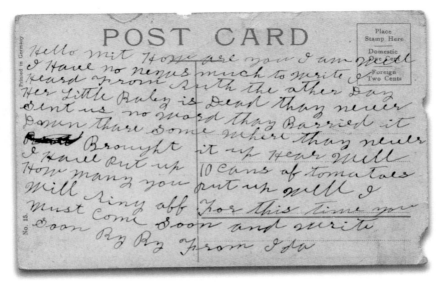

Ruth's Baby is Dead
Ida to Mittie

"Hello Mit how are you I am well I have no news much to write I heard from Ruth the other day her little baby is Dead thay never sent us no word thay barried it down thare some where thay never brought it up hear well I have put up 10 cans of tomatoes how many you put up well I will ring off for this time you must come soon and write soon by by from Ida"

Ruth Pruett was a sister to Ida. Ruth did not write letters to her siblings (or none survive if she did). While there is not much information on the baby that passed away, Ruth had three other sons and a daughter by her husband, Joseph Harris "Joe" Lynch, who ran a blacksmith shop that still stands as of 2019.

See page **163** for more information and a photo of Ruth.

CHAPTER TWO
A Hootin' Ole Time

W hile it was in a sense of humor that I poked fun at 'the good old days' having its flaws, there is no argument that people were still healthy, joyful, and able to have a fair share of pleasure and entertainment. As the next few letters show, people have not changed. While the tight posture, sour faces, strict nature, and rough'n'ready attitudes are prevalent in the period photographs and Hollywood movies available today, those are easily explainable. If video cameras had been invented 100 years prior to their time, we could know and see our ancestors to as quirky, amusing, and less alienated from ourselves. Photography was serious business—and expensive, too. People did actually smile, just not for the camera (usually). Thankfully, by the way of the pen, personality has prevailed where austere portraits have failed to display it.

The Pruett family had a tight-knit, affectionate relationship between one another. Lillie loved to dance, Ida loved to laugh, Alice loved her children, their mother Deleware loved—cats. John loved farming, Willie loved money, Joe loved—getting his jug full (of that good ol' mountain dew). Albeit, some interests were more reputable than others, but the love was still there yet.

Ida Pruett smiling, ca. 1910

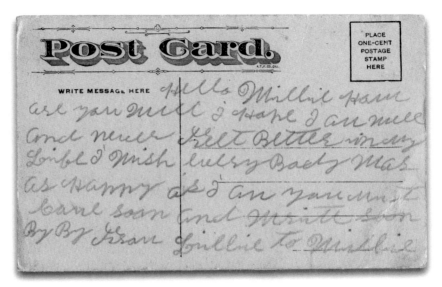

Happy as a Lark
Lillie to Willie

"Hello Willie how are you well I hope I am well and never felt better in my life I wish every body was as happy as I am you must come soon and write soon By By from Lillie to Willie"

Lillie is known to have been a merry soul and she loved to dance through the entirety of the night (as the further letters will show). She often remarked that she has never felt better. I wonder what kept her so happy.

Agoing to Beat You
Ida to Willie

"Hello Willie how are you I am well why hant you sent me a card before now I am agoing to beat you you have not sent me a postal in six months I got home to day I had a very nice time while I was gone Sallie brought me home to day I felt all right until he started back and then I had to cry after him Joe is gone to Danville a gain with a load of tobacco you must come soon write soon from Ida to Willie By By"

I'm unsure on who Sallie could be in relation to Ida. This letter confirms that Sallie was a man. Whether he was just a friend or someone that Ida went with, that is the mystery.

The city of Danville, Virginia was known as "The World's Best Tobacco Market" and served as the largest distributor of bright leaf tobacco in the state.

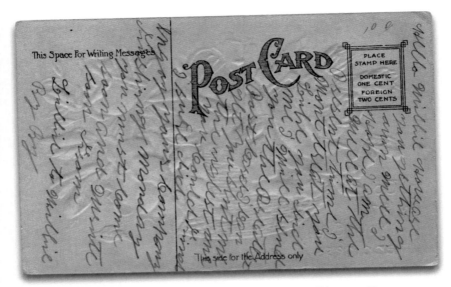

The Ugliest Post Card
Lillie to Willie

"Hello Willie how are you getting own well I hope I am well at the present time I wont treat you like you did me I will send you the prettiest post card I can get you sent me the uglest one you could find I sure did engoy your company fishing Monday you must come soon and write soon from Lillie to Willie By By"

Willie usually sent very plain cards, oftentimes featuring a bland rose or flower with no writing.

See page **151** for an example of a post card that tickles Lillie's fancy.

I Danced till 12
Lillie to Mittie

Hello Mittie how are you well I hope I am veary well this morning Mittie I wish you was up here with us today Joe is gone to Danville you just ought to bin with us the other night I danced till 12 well By By rite soon and come soon from Lillie

Joe and Lillie most likely gathered with friends and indulged in traditional step dances such as flatfooting, clogging, and/or buckdancing. While all are similar types of shoe-tapping jigs, the people of Appalachia will argue that there is a difference. In flatfooting, the feet are only moved straight up and down with light steps and no twists. Clogging has higher steps and focuses on tapping the toe instead of the heel. Buckdancing is the loudest and involves full body movement.

Pretty Boys
Sue to Ida

Hello Ida how are you hope you are well you ought to bin down at weal this week there was lots of pretty boys up there how is your garden chickens and flowers getting a long well by by for this time and rite soon from Susie to Ida

Ida attended the Weal Presbyterian Church in Chatham, Virginia. She was also known to have attended Marion Baptist Church down the road and the Hopewell United Methodist Church in Dry Fork, Virginia.

A Jubbelee Time
Ida to Aubrey

"Hello Aubrey how are you by this time no I dont I dont catch any rabbets but I buy me a rabbet some times I guess you have a jubbelee time over them rabbets that you catch harper said tell you to come down at xmas and talk to him some more you say you go to school you look like going to school you are not larg enough to go to school ha ha you must come and write soon from Ida here is a kiss for you"

Ida married Jessie Harper Kernodle, known to her as Harper, in 1915. They met through an article in a publication called The Companion, which offered a correspondence between single persons looking for friendship or relationship similar to dating websites of today. She and Harper were married for three years, though he passed away in 1918 from lung cancer due to excess dust inhalation. He made coffins and cabinets.
See the next page for a photo.

The postcard shown at top contains the following handwritten correspondence.

A Boy and his Billy Goat
Ida to Aubrey

"Hello Aubrey I am well how are you harper said tell you hello you ought to be down here you could have a good time playing a little boy that lives here next to me he is about your size got him a billy goat and a wagon Saturday he thinks lots of me he said that I could help him play with his goat you bet we will have a time with that goat ha ha you ought to be down here with me and the goat ha ha write soon here a kiss from Ida"

Jessie Harper Kernodle (1888-1918) Harper lived in Burlington, NC. Ida moved in with him and continued to live in Burlington for the rest of her life. She married again in 1920 to Jetson Pyle until his death in 1943 without having children.

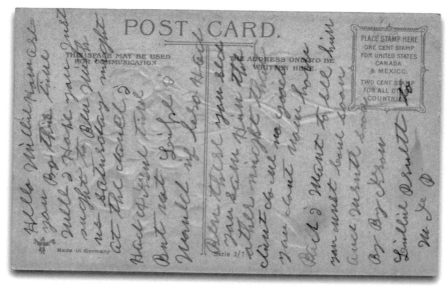

A Dance Without Bro
Lillie to Willie

"Hello Willie how are you by this time well I hope you just ought to ben with us saturday night at the dance I had a fine time but not like I would if bro had ben there you sed you saw him the other night that dint do me no good you dont now how bad I want to see him you must come soon and write soon by by from Lillie Pruett to W T P"

"Bro" refers to Joe Pruett.

Besides step dances, square dances were popular among group settings as well. They were held in homes or in public buildings. There was often one person known as a caller who directed the group as a whole to dance according to their call. For example, when to do-à-do (dance back to back). Although, that particular French phrase is pronounced as "dosey doe" due to rough English translation.

Delaware's Sun Bonnet 1

This sun bonnet was used while doing yardwork or even while attending church meetings. This one in particular has a longer 'skirt' to cover the shoulders. The style looks to be circa 1890's; although, sun bonnets like this were worn well into the 1930's.

CHAPTER THREE
Pullin' and Curin'

How many centuries does it take to grow and sell nearly eighty-five billion pounds of tobacco? In Danville, Virginia, it only takes one. The number 85,000,000,000 has more digits than a phone number with the area code included; this number comes only from stock sold during the span of the Danville Tobacco Association (which began in 1869). This was not simply tobacco, but the Rockefeller of tobacco species—bright leaf—which is unique to the Southern Virginia and upper North Carolina area.

Tobacco was not a job; it was a family tradition. Everyone participated, even toddlers who were too young to realize they were helping. Hands black and sticky from pulling leaves, smushing horrid looking green hornworms, the sweetened smell of a packed barn—these are ingrained memories that are universally shared among farming families.

The end of the War of 1861-1865 brought new life to the tobacco market. Cigarettes had only been introduced the decade prior, and demand was reaching for the sky.

"Holland's," "Graves," and "Planter's Warehouse" were some of the very first tobacco warehouses erected in Danville following the War of 1861-1865. Warehouses were gridded with endless piles and rows of cured tobacco leaves set out to be purchased. A limit was placed on the weight of each pile so that they could not exceed 300 pounds. Before the limit, some piles were known to weigh as much as 1,500 pounds.

800 Pounds of Bacca
Sue to Ida

"Hello Ida how are you by this hope you are well well we sold a load of tobacco yesday it weighed 8 hundred and brought too hundred and 15 dollars tell your mama she must make hast and come before it turns cold and you must come to stay a week soon well I have no news so by by tell all to come you come & rite soon from Sue"

$215 is equivalent to around $5,491 in 2019.

Auction Sale in Tobacco Warehouse, Danville, Virginia

Hundreds of piles of tobacco were set out for auction when brought to the warehouse. This is a look inside just one of the many warehouses in Danville.

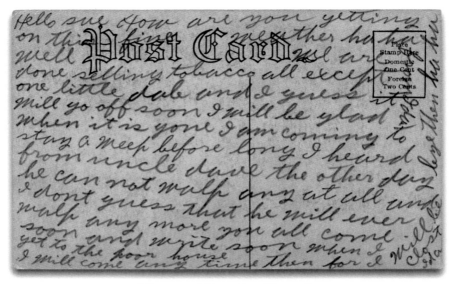

One Dab Left
Ida to Sue

"Hello Sue how are you getting on this fine weather ha ha well we are done selling tobacco all except one little dab and I guess it will go off soon I will be glad when it is gone I am coming to stay a week before long I heard from Uncle Dave the other day he can not walk any at all and I dont guess that he will ever walk any more you all come soon and write soon when I get to the poor house I will come any time then for I will be clost bye then ha ha Ida"

Uncle Dave refers to David D. Prewett, brother of Ida's father Ephraim Prewett. Dave was born in 1838 and served the Confederate Army in the 38th VA Infantry, Company D. This loss of mobility foreshadowed his forecoming death. He passed away on July 25, 1916.

11 Thousand Hills
Ida to Mittie

"Hello Mit I hope you are all well have you all planted any tobacco I have planted about 11 thousand hills how is your garden our little old garden is looking very well if it will keep on raining maybe I wont starve ha ha but I am getting very weak ha ha I tell you I am ha ha well you all must come real soon and write soon from Ida"

John owned 108 acres of land in Chatham, Virginia in which he, his brother Willie, and their wives Mittie and Sue grew tobacco, corn, tomatoes, beans, snaps, cabbage, and a wide array of other plants and flowers.

Crops Moast Dride
Willie to Delaware

"Hello mama how ar yo well I hope We ar all well we have had a nice rain and wind storm blowd down the corn froze sum tobacco leaves the crops wars moast dride up but I recken it will cum down soon I want to prime tobacco this weak write soon and come soon from Willie to Mamma"

It is obvious by this letter that spelling was not Willie's best subject. A wind storm blew down his corn crops and froze some of his tobacco, but they were beginning to dry up and were in need of rain, so the storm was useful for something.

"Priming tobacco" means to harvest the leaves that have matured enough to be prepared for drying in the barn.

Hello Aubrey I Hope you are well I Hope you can Help Daddy cure tobacco and Help Him catch Horns worms But Dont Let the worms toat you off thare is so many worms up Hear I am afraid to travle about well one of my Cats is Dead Cassey is all the cat I have now well you must come tell all the rest to come From Grand mother

Horns Worms
Delaware to Aubrey

"Hello Aubrey I hope you are well I hope you can help Daddy cure tobacco and help him catch horns worms but dont let the worms toat you off thare is so many worms up hear I am afrad to travle about well one of my cats is dead Cassey is all the cat I have now well you must come tell all the rest to come From Grand mother"

Tobacco Hornworms can destroy the entire crop if precautions are not taken. Like caterpillars, tobacco worms are still larvae and eventually endure a pupal stage in which they transform in to a large moth known as the hawk moth or hummingbird moth.

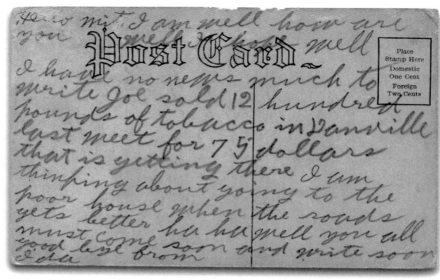

Going to the Poor House
Ida to Mittie

"Hello Mit I am well how are you well I hope well I have no news much to write Joe sold 12 hundred pounds of tobacco in Danville last week for 75 dollars that is getting there I am thinking about going to the poor house when the roads gets better ha ha well you all must come soon and write soon good bye from Ida"

$75 in this time is equivalent to around $1,980 in 2019.

Poorhouses were not just a joke, but a real location in many towns and cities across the U.S. Struggling families made a tight community in these buildings before the Federal Government involved itself in social welfare around the 1930's. Yet, few poorhouses still continued to exist, and a Virginia poor farm was still in operation as recently as 2014 in Maurertown, VA until a fire destroyed it.

3 Houses of Tobacco
Ida to Mittie

"Hello Mit how are you hope you are well are you all most done cutting tobacco we have cut 3 houses of tobacco and are agoing to cut anothing one tomorro well I have no news much to write you ought to have come last Sunday you could seen Mr Almond he paid me a visit last satday and Sunday well you all must come real soon and write soon by by from Ida"

In Virginia, tobacco is flue-cured, which simply involves the addition of a chimney to the tobacco barn. Venting the fire smoke away from the leaves enables the remaining moisture to escape. The interior of the barn is slowly raised to 100 degrees Fahrenheit until the leaves have yellowed and begin to wilt. The leaves must dry slowly to retain the best flavor. The temperature is raised to 130 until the bottom layer of leaves has dried, and then raised to 160 for the rest to dry.

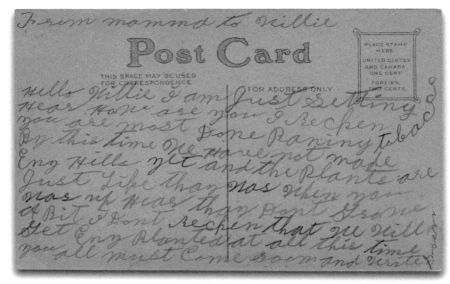

Thay Dont Grow a Bit
Delaware to Willie

"Hello willie I am just setting hear how are you I recken you are most done paning tobacco by this time we have not made eny hills yet and the plants are just like thay was when you was up hear thay dont growe a bit I dont recken that we will get eny planted at all this time you all must come soon and write soon from mamma to willie"

There are many factors that can prevent tobacco from growing correctly—a warm and dry April or May are prime time for planting, though there is still a chance of an unpredictable frost. Of course, weather too dry is damaging to the growth of the leaves, but so is weather too wet. Too much sun can lead to sunbaking, which turns the leaves into a spotty green and yellow color that is difficult to tend to.

A Curing of Tobacco
Willie to Delaware

"Hello mamma how ar you well I hope I have got a bile on my jaw and lener has got a bad coald I have no nuse to write except bad weather we soald a curing of tobacco at chatham last Friday for one hundred and aty ate dollers you must all cum soon and write soon from willie to mamma by "

$188 in this time is equivalent to around $4,963 in 2019.

The fire box and air curing method had been practiced since the year 1612, and it took between four to eight weeks to cure one barn of tobacco. Today, using the innovative gas-fueled method, the process has been cut down to one week.

Alice's Tobacco Planter

Before the mechanical hand setter tobacco planters were used, in came this piece of technology. To be fair, this can be used to plant any seeds, although many used it for tobacco as well. The pointed end is simply poked into the dirt to make a hole to plant seeds in. A useful word of advice is to find a planter which has an end that conforms comfortably to the palm of the hand, or else there shall be blisters. This 8 inch planter belonged to my great-great-grandmother Alice and it still has dirt on the end of it. This one is especially uncomfortable to grip, so I pity her for that. The more these planters are used, the smoother and shinier the wood becomes due to the oils of the hand soaking into the pores of the grain.

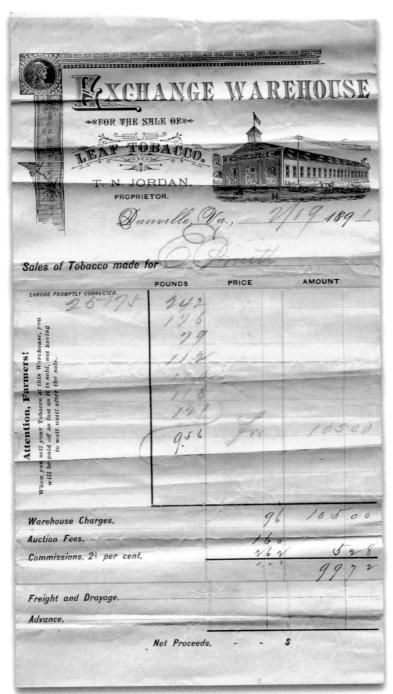

EXCHANGE WAREHOUSE

FOR THE SALE OF

LEAF TOBACCO.

T. N. JORDAN,
PROPRIETOR.

Danville, Va., 2/19 189 1

Sales of Tobacco made for E. Smith

	POUNDS	PRICE	AMOUNT
ERRORS PROMPTLY CORRECTED. 25175	242		
	126		
	79		
	112		
	116		
	141		
	956	Fr	10500

Attention, Farmers!

When you sell your Tobacco at this Warehouse, you will be paid off as fast as it is sold, not having to wait until after the sale.

Warehouse Charges,	96	10500
Auction Fees,	160	
Commissions, 2½ per cent,	262	528
	528	9972
Freight and Drayage,		
Advance,		
Net Proceeds, - - $		

Hezekiah Ford Pigg (1825-1908) was the owner and operator of the grandiose Pigg's Mill in Dry Fork, Virginia. Originally built in 1763 by his great-grandfather John Ghent Pigg (1716-1785), Heze ran the grain mill at full force from 1849 until his death in 1908, where it was then sold to Mr. J. H. Jones, who ran it until his death in 1944. The mill was last owned by Guy Lindsey Earles until it burned on January 8, 1953. All that is left today is a tall concrete storage bin and the water wheel. Heze married Martha Henry Rutledge in 1849 and had six children: Lysander Henry, Eliza "Bettie," David (infant death), John Hutchings "Hutch," Nannie, and William Ward Pigg. Hezekiah served in the Confederate Army—he enlisted as a corporal in the 38th VA Infantry, Company H in 1861, but received a disability discharge the following month. He reenlisted in 1864 and was captured at the Harper Farm in 1865 where he was held at Point Lookout, MD until June 16. He was 5ft 11in tall, had hazel eyes and brown hair. Heze served as Postmaster for his surrounding area known simply as Pigg's in 1889. The majority of Heze's descendants now live in California due to their collective migration from the county around 1908. Pittsylvania County historian and author Maude Carter Clement was the granddaughter of Hezekiah and Martha Pigg, who are both pictured at the left.

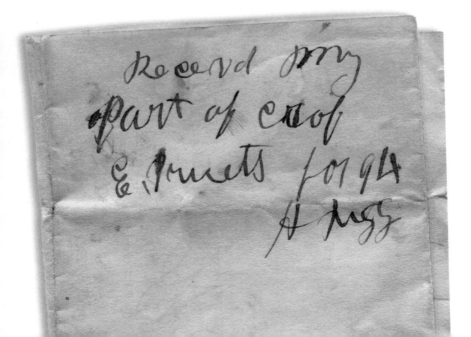

(Above) John Ballard Pruett, even in his older years, continued to raise tobacco. In this photo he stands proudly in his work overalls with his crop looming over head, leaves flopped over, just like his old hat. In his grasp, he has picked a particularly handsome leaf to display to the camera. This is an example of burley tobacco, which was used mainly for twisting into chewing tobacco and pipe tobacco.

Farmers' Alliance Warehouse,
FOR THE SALE OF LEAF TOBACCO.
OUR WORKING FORCE:

GENERAL MANAGER
J S. JOHNSTON, OF ROCKINGHAM COUNTY, N. C

BOOK-KEEPER
JOHN BUSTARD, OF HALIFAX COUNTY, VA.

FLOOR MANAGER
J. T. McGEE, OF CASWELL COUNTY, N C.

CLERKS
H. W COVINGTON, OF CASWELL COUNTY, N.C.
J T. MORTON, OF HALIFAX COUNTY, VA.

AUCTIONEER :
C. H. RICHMOND, OF PERSON COUNTY, N. C.

WEIGHMASTER :
T. D. BUSTARD, OF HALIFAX COUNTY, VA.

SOLICITOR :
J. W EVANS, OF PITTSYLVANIA COUNTY, VA.

BAGGAGEMASTER :
H M. LONG, OF PITTSYLVANIA COUNTY, VA.

Danville, Va., _____ 1892.

Sales made for _____ & _____

ERRORS CORRECTED.

No.	POUNDS.	PRICE.	AMOUNT
6 5 0	1 5 8	$ 5 4 8	$. 8 5 3
5 1	6 0	4 10	. 2 4 6
5 2	1 0 8	4 7 0	. 5 0 7
	3 2 6		

Warehouse Charges,	$ 1 6	$ 1 6 0 6
Auction Fees,	3 0	
Commission 2½ per cent.,	4 0	8 6
	$	$ 1 5 2 0
Freight and Drayage,		
Advances,		
Net proceeds,	$	

CHAPTER FOUR
Good Eatin'

Maters, taters, cornbread, cabbage, poke sallet, gravy, and biscuits. Grandmother *always* wears her apron. It's 95 degrees in the kitchen and she's still wearing long sleeves and has the wood stove fired up. She never uses any teaspoon, tablespoon, or cup measurements. When she's cooking, she means business—and there is no better cooking than Grandmother's.

People speak about "organic" and "homegrown" foods today—there was a time when those were the only types of foods available. Most southern meals were spared of any meats. The only time meats were eaten is if a chicken was butchered, father went hunting, or if someone killed hogs.

During my few years of 18th century living history, I have tasted meals prepared over a fire. While the finished product often looks wilder in appearance compared to the neat and uniform qualities of today's electric oven meals, the taste is much more alive. Wood adds to the taste—and it's a very welcoming addition.

What is a farm without a garden? Of course, while the mealtime palette of the last century was greatly restricted, they dined on the very foremost quality of their options—that is, if there was any food available. Garden food is seasonal; therefore, it is sometimes in abundance and requires help to eat the dozens of peaches and melons. Other times, the food runs quite short, and all that is left is the grease from the pan.

Howdedo Sue
Sue to Delaware

"Hello cousin Dellie how are you I hope you have not had no more chills and are well by this time Willie said he would rite next week and cousin Susie Hutson said tell you howdedo My snaps has begun to bloom I guess I will have something to ate before long well I will ring off you must come soon and rite soon from S to Cousin Dellie by by"

"Susie Hutson" refers to Mary Susan Giles (1860-1935). She was the wife of George L. Hutson and the mother of Nannie Hutson, (1886-1962) who is mentioned often as a close friend to the family.

Sue refers to her mother-in-law as her cousin, which is true. Sue's father David Harris Watson is the first cousin to Delaware. They also both come from the Giles family, which is where "cousin Susie" comes into play. Susie is the daughter of Thomas Hill Giles. Sue and Susie are double third cousins.

Sallet to Cook
Ida to Sue

"Hello Susin by the way how are you I am getting on nice and right you said that you had plenty of sallet to cook I wonder if sallet is all you got you never said enything a bout having nothing els I wanted to come down there but if sallet is all you got I dont want to come well I will ring off come real soon write soon from Ida to Susin By By"

"Sallet" refers to two things: it can refer to poke sallet (and "sallet" is the correct term, which is more archaic English), or turnip greens. In this case, it refers to poke sallet, which is a plant that can be toxic if not cooked correctly.

Pokeweed
photo from wildabundance.net

A Bigg Supper To Night
Delaware to Nina

"Hello Nina how are you by this time I am getting on veary well to night Joe got home from Danville Sund in the evening and brought me a bag of cheese and I eat a bigg supper to night cheese and stewed chicken I wish you had ben up hear to tack supper with me tell Lillie we are are getting on fine up hear tell her to do what you tell her to do and dont be lazy well you must come soon and wright soon by by from Grand mother"

People in the South today often pronounce the word "Sunday" as "Sundee," which justifies Delaware spelling the word as "Sund" in this letter. The same goes for pronunciations of the other days of the week, "Mundee, Tuesdee, Winsdee," etc.

By "tack" she means to say "take."

Maby We Wont Starve

Sue to Ida

"Hello Ida how are you and all the rest getting on well I hope we are all up I have no news to rite only I have a fresh cow and my garden looks fairly well maby we wont starve I would like to see that picture you must excuse this old card maby I can do better next time you must come & rite soon tell your mother she must come soon so by by tell Lillie she must come from Sue"

By the time of this letter, Ida and Sue lived around six and a half miles away from each other. Ida lived with her mother, Delaware, on modern day Irish Road diagonal to Dame Memorial Church. Sue lived on Hickory Road in Chatham with her husband, Willie Pruett, her sister, Mittie, and Mittie's husband, John Ballard Pruett. Both areas are considered part of Chatham today, although Ida's area used to be known as Wilmer and was part of Dry Fork, Virginia.

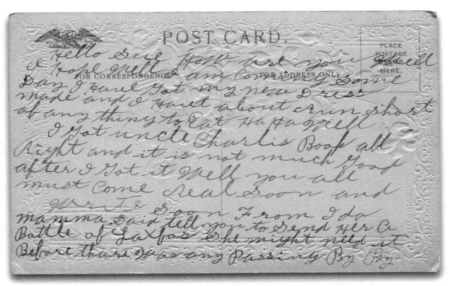

New Dress, No Food
Ida to Sue

"Hello Sue how are you well I hope well I am coming some day I have got my new dress made and I have about run short of any thing to eat ha ha well I got Uncle Charlis book all right and it is not much good after I got it well you all must come real soon and write soon from Ida Mamma said tell you to send her a bottle of Laxfos she might need it before thare was any passing By By"

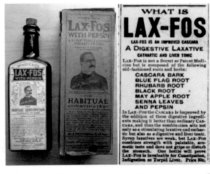

photos from worthpoint.com and chroniclingamerica.loc.gov

Winstead's Lax-Fos with Pepsin for Habitual Constipation was a laxative. The company was mainly situated in the south and was bought out in 1916.

Canning Tomatoes
Sue to Ida

"Hello Ida how are you by this time well I hope we are all most run down down here they have cured one house of leavs and are putting more have you pulled any up there I have put up 22 cans of tomatoe evry thing is getting verry dry down there well you must come and rite real soon from Sue"

Tomato plants require weeks of tender love and care in order to grow healthily and plentifully. Although, when the tomatoes are ripe, they all seem to be ripe at once, so there's always a bountiful supply. How does one put them all to use without letting them rot? by canning, of course.

Plenty to Ate
Mittie to Ida

"Hello Ida how are you hope all is well we have not had any rain since your mother was here have you had any rain up there we have plenty to ate just now cabbage snaps potatoes tomatoes corn and butter beans well you must come soon & write soon tell Alice hello for me tell her I think of her these hot days from Mit"

Of course, "your mother" refers to Delaware.

Alice lived beside her mother, Delaware, for a few years before moving further into Dry Fork, which is why there aren't many letters by her. She only began to send letters once she moved a little over five miles away around 1912 to work on a farm on modern day Hylton Lane. She bought her own house soon after.

Judging Peaches
Lillie to Willie

"Hello Willie how are you well I hope I am well at the present time I guess you are most done selling tobacco by this time aint you you better let me judge peaches for you for I always pick the sweatest ones I can find so by by write soon and come soon from Lillie C Pruett to Willie T Pruett"

According to a blog by Frog Hollow Farm, the best peaches are characterized by:

1.) a deep gold background color; the red color does not matter

2.) it is quite soft by test of a gentle squeeze

3.) wrinkles and shriveled skin around the stem

Out of the Butter Biness
Ida to Sue

"Hello Sue how are you by this time well I hope well xmas will soon bee hear get your ready for it well I have no news to tell you we have got eggs to make out with for xmas but we are out of the butter biness I dont milk now at all well you all must come soon write soon wish you a marry xmas and a happy new year by by from M I"

If there was fresh milk available, it was placed in a cool location in a setting dish for around 12 hours for the cream to rise to the top. After it is clearly risen, (like oil on water) the cream is skimmed off of the top and placed into a churn. There are several types of churns, but the one Ida used most likely resembled a slender barrel with a plunger on the top. Through constant motion, the yellow fat floats up from the buttermilk and hardens into butter once it is strained of water.

Dont Wake Me Up
Ida to Sue

"Hello Sue I hope you are well Sue you ought to come to day miss nannie spent the day with us ha ha well sue I have plenty to eat now if you will step up hear some bright night I guess you can get you a bag full of peas and corn but dont make no norse to wake me up ha ha alice is well thay was all hear to day well you all come soon I am coming when I get done cutting tobacco write soon from ida by by"

by "norse," she means "noise."

See page **60** for more information on *Miss Nannie*.

Ida and her mother lived on 20 acres of land. The Lewis Cassidy Giles store served as their local general store and post office. Knowing Ida, her garden was most likely as big as she could possibly make it.

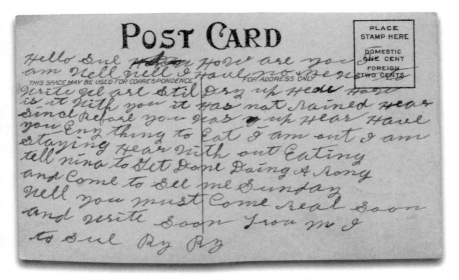

Staying Without Eating
Ida to Sue

"Hello Sue how are you I am well well I have no news to write we are stil dry up here how is it with you it has not rained hear since before you was up hear have you eny thing to eat I am out I am staying hear with out eating tell nina to get done doing a rong and come to see me Sunday well you must come real soon and write soon from M I to Sue by by"

Just as there were times when food was in abundance, there were plenty of times where it was hard to find. This is the reason that so many neighbors looked after each other and shared plentifully. Survival was a job, so some days there was just no food to eat.

Eating Candy Till Perserved
Ida to Mittie

"Hello Mit I am well hope you are the same well I have no news well cousin John has not been back to see me any more ha ha I have just been setting hear eating candy till I am almost perserved ha ha well you all must come soon I am coming to stay a week some day well come and write soon from Ida"

Ida humors us yet again when she remarks that she is nearly preserved, which is in reference to how pears, figs, apples, and other fruits can be made into savory preserves such as jams and jellies using sugar as the main preservative.

Maybe this is the reason she is always so upbeat and witty.

"Sunbeam's" Candy Bag

Imagine filling up this penny candy bag as a child with some of the only sugar treats you'll get to eat for months. Surely this bag felt just as crisp as a $100 bill. The "Sunbeam's" candy design was patented in 1906, so this bag is from somewhere near the years following. I'm unsure which Pruett family member it belonged to exactly—probably a young one.

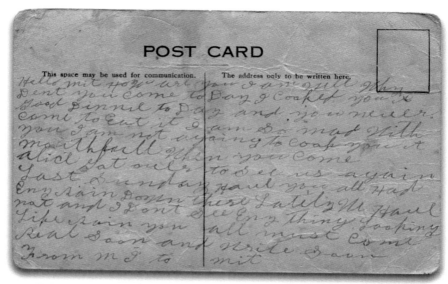

Not Agoing to Cook for You
Ida to Mittie

"Hello Mit how are you I am well why dent you come to day I cooked you a good dinnie to day and you never come to eat it I am so mad with you I am not agoing to cook you a mouthfull when you come Alice got over to see us again last Sunday have you all had eny rain down there lately we have not and I dont see eny thing looking like rain you all must come real soon and write soon from M I to Mit"

I can imagine this whole circumstance—I see Ida waiting for Mittie to arrive, but ultimately giving up and eating her cold food in a peeved manner and then scribbling this letter out to her. This letter is definitely not as fierce as it may seem. I could not see Ida letting this bother her for more than a moment.

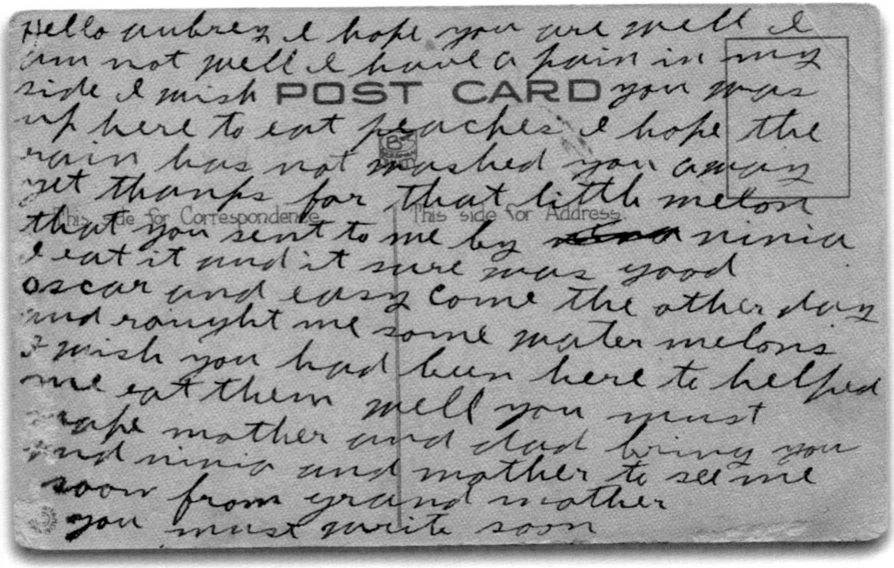

[Handwritten postcard:]

Hello aubrey I hope you are well I am not well I have a pain in my side I wish POST CARD you was up here to eat peaches I hope the rain has not washed you away yet thanks for that little melon that you sent to me by ~~~~ ninia I eat it and it sure was good oscar and easy come the other day and rought me some water melons I wish you had been here to helped me eat them well you must ape mother and dad bring you and ninia and mother to see me soon from grand mother you must write soon

Help Eat Water Melons
Delaware to Aubrey

"Hello Aubrey I hope you are well I am not well I have a pain in my side I wish you was up here to eat peaches I hope the rain has not washed you away yet thanks for that little melon that you sent to me by ninia I eat it and it sure was good Oscar and Casy come the other day and brought me some water melons I wish you had been here to helped me eat them well you must make mother and dad bring you and ninia and mother to see me soon from grandmother you must write soon"

Oscar and Cassie are two of Alice's children. Cassie was born in 1906 and Oscar in 1908. The pictures below show what they looked like around the time of this letter.

Cassie (left) and Oscar Meadows (right) circa 1911

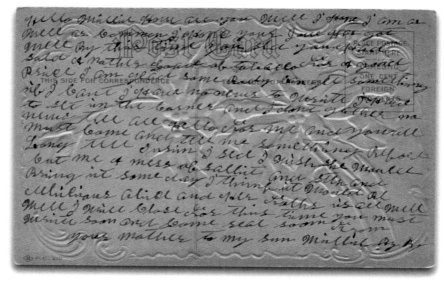

A Mess of Sallit
Delaware to Willie

"Hello Willie how are you well I hope I am as well as common I hope your jaw has got well by this time you sed you had sold a nother load of tobacco for a good price I am glad some body can get something if I cant I have no news to write I have to set in the corner and I dont gather no news tell all hello for me and you all must come and tell me something before long tell Susin I sed I wish she would cut me a mess of sallit and step and bring it some day I think it would be delicioius Alice and her folks is all well well I will close for ths time you must write soon and come real soon from your mother to my sun Willie by by"

It seems that Delaware loved her cut of sallet, but Ida grew fairly tired of it as shown on page **61**.

Plenty of Greace to Eat
Ida to Mittie

"Hello Mit I hope that you are well I guess that you are ready for xmas I am about ready I have killed hogs and I have got plenty of greace to eat ha ha our hogs waid 569 Have you all kiled yours well you see I have got my stocking hung up I would like to get you to fill it for me if you will ha ha well you all must come and write soon from Ida"

This was the time when families utilized hogs for "everything but the oink." Grease was extracted from the hog and used later in frying foods to add flavor to it. Kitchens usually had a grease jar for quick access when cooking. My grandmother, Margaret, still has a grease jar that I've seen her use in her cooking.

The Cabbage is Dead
Delaware to Aubrey

"Hello Aubrey I hope you are well if you can go to Chatham and stay all day I know you can come to see me tell mother and daddy to bring you to see me soon I got the laxfos all right well the cabbage plants are all dead in the bead but 2 are 3 and the most of them that we planted is dead tell uncle willie I hope his bad cold has got well tell him to come soon and bring aunt sue to see me you all come soon and write soon from grand mother"

See page **64** for more information on *Laxfos*.

In case there is some trouble reading this sentence, "the cabbage plants are all dead in the bead but 2 are 3" she is saying that all of the cabbage plants are dead in the plant bed except for 2 or 3 of them.

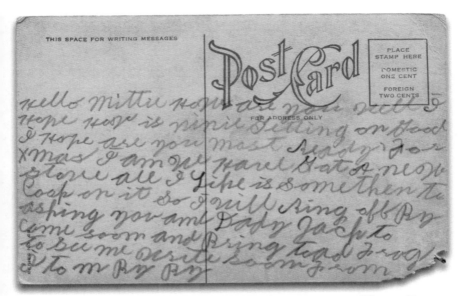

New Stove, Nothing to Cook

Ida to Mittie

"Hello Mittie how are you well I hope how is ninie getting on good I hope are you most ready for xmas I am we have got a new stove all I like is somethen to cook on it so I will ring off by asking you and dady Jack to come soon and bring Toad Frog to see me write soon from I to M by by"

I assume that Toad Frog was a nickname for baby Aubrey. I do not know the story behind the name, but I'm sure he either learned to make frog noises or liked finding frogs.

Cook stoves of the time were made of cast iron and weighed hundreds of pounds. Chopped wood was always stored close by and the fire had to be tended to throughout the day. Wood stoves served as a place to cook meals, warm up bath water, and warm the house in winter.

Hog Killin'
The Tradition and Process

The hog is fat and looks to bear the fruit of fine dining. A hog was not a family meal, but a neighborhood delicacy. Usually, a hog that was born during the Spring was killed once the first frost of the year was about to take place. Colder weather meant that the meat could be well-preserved since there lacked the reliability of a refrigerator. If lucky, the preserved meat could last a full year without expiring through salting.

Once the selection had been made, the hog was taken down by way of a clean shot just between the eyes (of course, the hog must be dead in order to cook it). It was then strung up on a tree or other sturdy foundation to drain of blood through a cut in the neck. This process is known as bleeding. Often, the blood was saved to make foods such as black pudding (congealed blood), pig blood cake, and other wholesome meals.

The hog was then put into a trough of boiling water to scald off any of the hair and clean the skin. While the skin was still brittle, it was scraped using a round knife resembling a jar lid in order to get rid of the rest of the prickly bristles, then it was dipped once again into the boiling water.

Next, the hog was gutted. The organs were removed and saved, of course, for yet another list of delicacies to be eaten in the near future. The real prize of the kill was the intestines, which provided casings for sausage. Of course, the ears, feet, and tongue were saved as well. The hams were saved for later smoking over hickory or similar woods. The skin makes a fantastic crunchy treat as well—hard as can be, though surprisingly flavorful.

After all of the interior had been removed, the rest of the hog was butchered.

For a more in-depth look at this process, I highly recommend the book *Notes of a Time Traveler: Our Forgotten Folk Heritage* by Joe Lively.

(Above) Hog Killing in Virginia, ca. 1939 - Photo from Appalachian
Magazine
(Below) Using an ash hopper to make lye from rendered lard for use in
soap - Photo from candidslice.com

Above: "9/12/12 Eggs 25c chix 16 shoes Elliotts Store Hopewell R2"

Below: "9/22/12 Come and see our new line dry goods notions & shoes next week Elliotts Store"

... Compliments of ...

The Little Mercantile Co.
ELLIOTT'S STORE
GENERAL MERCHANDISE
and GENTS' FURNISHINGS
DRY FORK   R. F. D. No. 2

Above is most likely the top part of a calendar. The exact year is unknown, but it is most likely from around 1910. Elliott's Store was also known as "The Little Mercantile Company." It stood on Dry Fork Road beside where Hopewell United Methodist Church is today.

Elliott's Store
Dry Fork, Virginia

J ust before the turn of the 20th century, two brothers, Robert Eldridge Elliott (1868-1955) and Wesley Carrington "Carr" Elliott (1871-1968) began construction on a new store. Shortly after the first building was erected, it was turned into a blacksmith shop and the brothers built a bigger store, which is depicted above by a pencil drawing I did in 2018. Carr shoed mules and horses, fixed wagons, and ran the mercantile store.

A man named Charlie Washington Grant came to Dry Fork from Franklin County and began to work at Elliott's Store in 1909. Just a few years after, he married Carr's daughter, Estelle "Essie" Elliott and they had three children: Ruth, Hazel, and Garnett Grant. Unfortunately, Essie passed away in 1918 at the young age of 23. Her daughter Hazel passed away in 1919, and her son Garnett in 1920, leaving Ruth Grant as the only child left. In 1921, Charlie married a younger sister of Essie's named Nannie Lou Elliott. It was custom for a widower to marry their late wife's sister. Together, they had four children: Christine, Howard Carrington,

Granville Morrison "Joe," and Garland Grant.

In 1944, Charlie bought the store for himself and renamed it to Grant's Store. It was the center market of Dry Fork, comparable to the Wal-Mart of today. Charlie passed away in 1953 and his son Garland took authority over the store. Anyone over 50 who has grown up in Dry Fork surely knows of Garland and Ruth Grant's true and honest dealings. Garland took down the original building and constructed a new one in the early 1960's that still stands today. In 1977, Grant's Store closed, and the keys were handed to new buyers. Since then, it has been a few other grocery stores, a Butcher's Block, and it is currently for sale again.

Garland and Ruth were second cousins to my great-grandfather, George Grant. I also come from the Elliott family twice.

My drawing depicts the store as Grant's Store with Ruth on the left, Garland in the doorway, and their father Charlie standing at the front.

Wesley Carrington "Carr" Elliott and his wife Mary "Sue" Price circa 1894

Charlie Washington Grant circa 1903

CHAPTER FIVE
Home Gossip

W here were you born—at a hospital or at home? In the year 1910, over 95% of babies were born at home with no modern epidurals, analgesics, or tranquilizers. The homeplace was a source of countless events both exciting and lackluster. Telephones only existed in a mere 8% of homes, most of which were in city limits. Bathtubs were installed in a whopping 14% of homes, also mostly in city limits. For farming families, the home was mightily humble.

When the Internet wasn't even upon its foundation of being considered, and when the family home was miles from a city or town, the neighborhood was quite earnestly the world for that family. How are the neighbors? How are the kids? How's the cat? There wasn't much more to inquire.

Solitude was expensive—most farming households were small log structures built by hand. They had few rooms with many occupants. Though, the large families were necessary for more help with raising tobacco crops and tending to the horses, cattle, and hogs. While the workday was long, there was still downtime. There was time to craft, time to create, time to sew, time to quilt, and time to build.

This was the time when mail was delivered to the local general store. Envelopes were addressed to the recipient and town name, sometimes followed by road number. The mail was delivered to the nearest post office or store that acted as the post office, and that's where it was picked up.

Plenty of Cats
Delaware to Nina

"Hello Nina how are you I dont feal no better than I did when you was hear you and aunt Sue and uncle Willie must come soon before the weather get two cold it is getting pretty cold up hear now well I got my wheat in the ground before it rained Nina one of my cats is sick but if it dies I will have plenty without it well you all must come soon write soon from Grandmother"

How many cats is plenty? That's almost concerning, but it is still relatable. The trait of attracting cats must have been hereditary because my great-grandmother, Louise, can be seen in quite a few photos posing with various cats that just happened to arrive at her house. As a child, I remember seeing three stray cats that lingered around our land, same as they had been for decades.

"Nina" is actually pronounced as "N-eye-na" instead of "N-ee-na."

Going to School
Alice to Delaware

[Jan 30 1914]
    "Hello Mother how are you well I hope We are all well as common well I have no news to tell you Nettie and Cassie is going to school and I get very lones I looked for you and Joe yestday but I dident see you plese write soon and come soon from alice to mother"

Nettie and Cassie most likely went to Piedmont School in Dry Fork, VA. Nettie only completed first grade and her sister Cassie completed second grade. Oscar and Louise had the highest educations of the bunch, which was third grade.

Nettie (left) and Cassie Meadows (right) circa 1911

Meadows School Books

Shown above are a selection of school books that were used by the children of Alice. They are as follows: *New-World Health Series Book 1 - Primer of Hygiene Revised Edition* by John W. Ritchie, 1915; *The Test and Study Speller - Complete Book* by Daniel Starch and George A. Mirick, 1921; and *Modern Primary Arithmetic* by David Eugene Smith, 1914. Also included are a slate board and a leather book strap, The school books were passed down to each sibling as they went through the corresponding grade. Nettie, Cassie, Oscar, Louise, and Joseph Meadows used these books and wrote his or her name in the book, all of which are showcased on the following page.

Nettie Meadows

Cassie Meadows

Oscar Meadows

Louise Meadows

Joseph Meadows

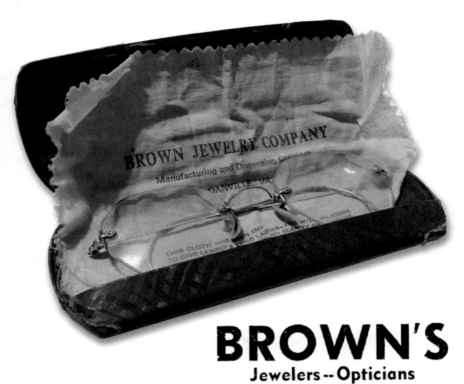

BROWN'S
Jewelers -- Opticians
437 Main St. — Masonic Temple — Downtown Danville

Alice's Glasses
Brown Jewelry Company Danville VA

Alice bought these glasses from the Brown Jewelry Company in Danville, Virginia, which was founded by M. R. D. Brown in August 1919. In 1922, the company moved into the lobby of the 'new' Masonic Temple that still stands as of 2019. The glasses seem to be from the 1930's or '40's.

Cold Anough for Snow
Ida to Sue

"Hello Sue I am glad to know that you are hanging on yet ha ha I am afraid that you will have to stand some more snow ha ha for it is cold anough now to be snowing well Alice and her childern are well some of the childern has had the chicken pox and are well now and the rest has not taken them yet well you all come soon and write soon bring the childern with you when you come Ida"

Chicken Pox is an infection that has only become relatively subdued in the past 25 years. Of course, it served as more of a scare to be infected with the Chicken Pox during a time when a very similar looking pandemic disease, Smallpox, was sweeping the nation unrelentlessly. While it is not usually a dire situation for children to have the Chicken Pox, there is still a possibility of death, although the death rate is less than one per cent.

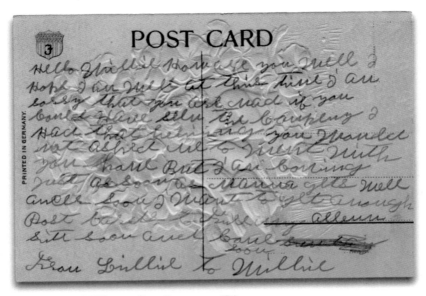

Hevining Company
Lillie to Willie

"Hello Willie how are you well I hope I am well at this time I am sorry that you are mad if you could have seen the company I had that hevining you would not asked me to went with you shaw but I am coming just as soon as mamma gets well ancer soon I want to get anough post cards to fill my album rite soon and come soon from Lillie to Willie"

[*on the back*]
"Come the third Sunday and I will go with you home if I can and thay have got over the mumps"

"shaw" is a spelling of the expression "pshaw," which is a declaration of disapproval or contempt. The first recorded use of "pshaw" was in 1607 and is still used throughout the southern United States.

See page **22** for more information about using the prefix 'h-' in front of the word 'evening.'

Also, see page **159** for the other side of this card.

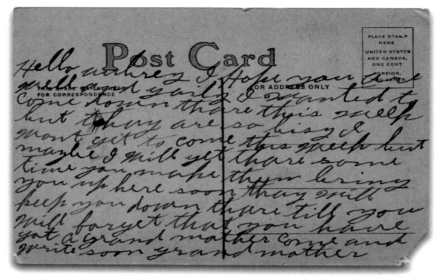

Don't Forget Grandmother
Delaware to Aubrey

"Hello Aubrey I hope you are well and gaily I wanted to come down thare this week but thay are so hisy I wont get to come this week but maybe I will get thare some time you make them bring you up here soon thay will keep you down thare till you will forget that you have got a grandmother come and write soon from grandmother"

At the time of Delaware's death in 1915, she was a grandmother to 14 grandchildren; she had 23 in all. Her first, Robert Green "Bobby" Meadows (below left), was born in 1895 and her last, Phillip Jones, (below right) was born in 1934. Delaware's last surviving grandchild, Jerleen "Jerri" Jones Mason of Danville, VA, passed away in 2018.

Big Sack Full of Kisses
Ida to Aubrey

"Hello Aubrey I hope you are well I am glad that you can read in your new book thank you little boy for that bundle of kisses we appreachated them very much for they was sweet kisses harper said tell you to send him a big sack full of kisses next time ha ha well you all must come soon and write soon good bye be a good little boy here is a kiss for you from Ida"

See page **40** for more information on *Harper*.

By this time, Ida had moved to Burlington, North Carolina with her husband, Harper Kernodle.

As much as Ida loved children, she never had any of her own. Whether it was her own preference or natural misfortune, it intrigues me to imagine knowing her children and further descendents.

Baby Scribble
Nina or Aubrey to Grandmother

The two post cards to the left are quite unique, in that, they were 'written' by the babies themselves. These letters of loving intention were scrawled out by either Nina or her brother Aubrey Pruett. Who knows what they were meant to say; though, I am sure that the baby knew clear as day. Above are photos of Nina (left) and Aubrey (right) both circa 1911.

The War and Corn Shuckings
Delaware to Nina

"Hello Ninia I hope you are well I am not well I hope you and mother will come to see me before the weather getts too cold I have no news to write about all that I hear is about the war and corn shuckings I would have looked for you all Sunday if it had not been raining when any of you all comes you can bring me a bottle of laxfos I am not out yet but if I live I guess I will want some more Well tell all of them hello for me and you all must come soon and write soon from Grandmother"

This letter was written soon after the beginning of World War I, which started in Europe within the weeks following the assassination of Austrian-Hungarian Archduke Franz Ferdinand on July 28, 1914. There was a constant flow of war-related articles in local newspapers at this time.

See page **64** for more information on *Laxfos*.

John's Corn Husking Peg

This husking peg is used by putting three fingers into the strap and the pointer finger into the more durable piece at the front. The peg is then slid down the ear of corn while still attached to the stalk, which splits the husk and allows the ear to easily be removed and thrown into the wagon. Normally, husking pegs lack the front section where the pointer finger goes. Less ornate husking pegs are simply a nail with a leather strap attached.

In the year 1900, Americans planted approximately 95,000 acres of corn, many of which were completely husked by hand.

I Have the Toothache
Nina to Delaware

"Hello grandmother how are you well I hope I am having the toothache every day and mama & aunt sue is both on the grunts we hope you have got well so you can come to see us soon we want to come up there soon as we can you all must come and rite soon from Nina"

The fact that Nina was having toothaches every day influences me to believe that she was probably young enough to still be teething. If that is the case, it would place the year of this card in 1910 since she was born the year prior.

Meating at the Old Mountain

Ida to Sue

"Hello Susin how are you getting on I am well I hope your year has got well by this time I went to the meating at the old mountain yestday I had a veary good old time up there I saw more people up there than I ever saw before tell willie that Sallie was the best looking one that was on the ground well you must come real and write soon by by from I to Susin"

The meeting that Ida is referring to is most likely a Methodist tent revival meeting that was held somewhere around White Oak Mountain in Dry Fork, Virginia instead of at the church.

tent revival meeting circa 1915
picture from The Asbury Journal

Sleeping on Palets
Nina to Delaware

"Hello grandmother how are you I hope you are well I wint to weal today and had a good time Aubrey and I are sleeping on our palets while mama is riting our cards well grandma you must come soon as you can we are coming up there soon rite soon from Nina"

In reference to Nina's sleeping pallet, this most likely was a simple sack (a tick) sewn together, made of cotton, filled with straw and placed directly onto the floor.

While it is obvious that neither Nina or Aubrey could proficiently write letters during the lifetime of their grandmother Delaware, this letter confirms that their mother, Mittie, wrote their letters for them.

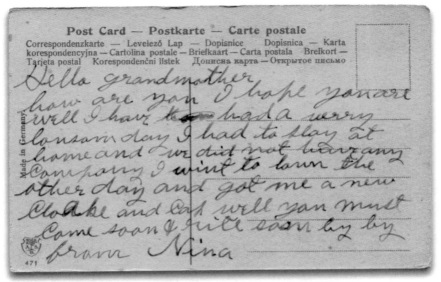

New Cloake and Cap
Nina to Delaware

"Hello grandmother how are you I hope you are well I have had a verry lonsom day I had to stay at home and we did not have any company I wint to town the other day and got me a new cloake and cap well you must come soon & rite soon by by from Nina"

The price of clothing in this time period seems like a joke compared to what is found in the twenty-first century due to massive inflation. For comparison, using my x3 great-grandfather William Osborne Meadows's tab from a store in Callands, Virginia from 1913, he bought 1 shirt for 50 cents, 1 pair of pants for $1.50, and 1 pair of shoes for $1.75.

Quilted and Hemed

Ida to Sue

"Hello Sue how are you I am fealing all right I have put in a bed quilt to day and quilted it out and hemed it and it is not bed time yet and I went from home and spent the day it is telling what I could have done if I had sayed at home to day ask Willie why it is that he cant send me a post card some time tell him he is getting two bigg for his old hat I will see a bout him when I come down there well you all must come real soon write soon by by from M I"

The whole family loved quilting, and that's how my great-grandmother Louise made her extra money. Louise's sister Nettie was also renowned for her quilts, and that's what all of the newborn babies got from her. Below is a quilt that was handmade by Nettie Meadows, a daughter of Alice.

Stayed Home so Long
Ida to Sue

"Hello Sue I hope you are well I have no news to write wish I was down thare I have stayed at home so long if I was to get away I would not know how to behave myself dont you know I had a card from cousin Nannie the other day she said she would not be back down thare for any thing ha ha what would you all down thare give to have her back ha ha you all must come soon write soon from Ida"

See page **60** for more information on *Cousin Nannie*.

Surely Ida had been bored out of her mind. As if it was not bad enough that there was no television, radio, or telephone, she lived on a farm with nothing around it but livestock. Most of the time, all there was to do was to read the Bible or sew something.

Mama Made a Dress
Nina to Delaware

"Hello grandmother how are you by this I hope you are better I dont feel well at all but I can pick up chips for mama and feed the chickens mama is making me a dress and I am goin to ware it up there when we come you must come soon as you get well enough from Nina write soon"

What brand of clothing did people wear in the past? Mother's brand. Before the time of mass machine production and "one-size fits all," it was just easier for mother or grandmother to make clothes herself. Take note that this was also a time period when traditional roles called for women to be housewives. When most people only had two to four outfits to their name, it was imperative to know how to sew and repair clothing.

A Sore Thumb
Ida to Mittie

"Hello Mit how are you by this time better I hope I receaved your cataloge and post card all right was glad to hear from you but I was sorry to hear that your thumb had got in such a shape I heard you speak about your thumb when I was there and said it was sore but I never thought a bout it getting so bad I truely hope it is better by this time tell nina I wish she was up hear to sing casey jones for me well I will stop you must let me hear how your thumb is I can read your left hand writing all right from M I to Mit"

Whatever the cause of Mittie's thumb injury was, it ultimately resulted in the loss of a joint in her thumb.

Casey Jones is a popular railway folk ballad based on a true story from 1900. Its first chorus goes as follows:

"Casey Jones--mounted to the cabin
Casey Jones--with his orders in his hand
Casey Jones mounted to the cabin, and he took
his farewell trip to that Promised Land."

Make her a Squart Gunn
Ida to John

"Hello John I am well how are you and how is ninie getting on can she walk if she can it is time you was makig her that squart gunn why ant you tenden the meaten at marrin I was down ther Friday night I never saw none of you all but I saw Fred Goad and all right you all must and visit soon from I to J by by"

The spelling in this letter is very phonetic. "why ant you tenden the meaten at marrin" means "why ain't you attending the meeting at Marion?" Marion is the church that Ida went to.

Before squirt guns were actually in the shape of guns, they were metal cylinders with a pump. This is most likely the type John would have made for his daughter:

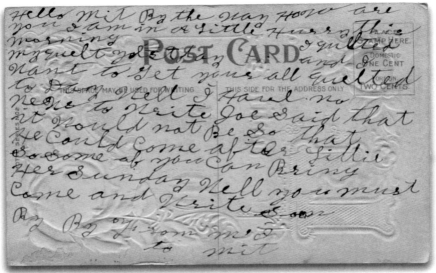

Quilting for Everyone
Ida to Mittie

"Hello Mit by the way how are you I am in a little hurry this morning I quilted my quilt yestday and I want to get your all quilted to day well I have no news to write Joe said that it would not be so that he could come after Lillie so some of you can bring her Sunday well you must come and write soon by by from M I to Mit"

It can take hundreds of hours to sew a quilt by hand depending on the size. A sewing machine can drastically cut the process to—*just* a couple dozen hours! The point is that quilting takes quite a long time, so it is definitely worth being the main subject of a letter. Quilts are a special type of warmth, and this poem says it well:

We're covered by a quilt of love,
It warms us like no other.
God used the hands of one so dear,
The one we call Grandmother
*   -unknown*

Hopewell Church
Sue to Ida

"Hello Ida how are you by this time I do not feel so verry well I hope you are all well have you bin tending the meeting at Hopewell and how does brother Carson preach by now I must come soon and rite soon tell your mother and Lillie they must come by by from Sue"

Hopewell United Methodist Church was founded on land granted by Hezekiah Pigg in 1878. Before it was a physical building, the location was used for brush arbor meetings, which were religious revivals where people camped for days or weeks. Brush arbors are named for the fact that they were normally held under shelters made of leafy branches fastened overtop of a pole structure.

Willie's Bible

This little 5 inch by 3.5 inch New Testament Bible belonged to Willie Pruett. The inside cover holds his signature and the title page is dated from the year 1885.

CHAPTER SIX
A r o u n d   t h e   F a r m

Farm life revolved heavily around day-to-day rigmarole and scheduling. Think a 9:00 AM to 5:00 PM job is troublesome? Most farming families of the past completed what modern Americans would consider a day's work before 9:00 AM even arrived. The following text is taken from a firsthand account of a farm wife from around the year 1900, written in her own hand:

> "Any bright morning in the latter part of May I am out of bed at four o'clock; next, after I have dressed and combed my hair, I start a fire in the kitchen stove, and while the stove is getting hot I go to my flower garden and gather a choice, half-blown rose and a spray of bride's wreath, and arrange them in my hair, and sweep the floors and then cook breakfast.
>
> While the other members of the family are eating breakfast I strain away the morning's milk (for my husband milks the cows while I get breakfast), and fill my husband's dinner pail, for he will go to work on our other farm for the day.
>
> By this time it is half-past five o'clock, my husband is gone to his work, and the stock loudly pleading to be turned into the pastures."

Vivacious pride was taken in both the practical nature and elegance of the house and farm's land. Ornamental flower arrangements were often planted, spotless from weeds, and clever in their arrangement. Horses were kept clean, their hooves often shoed, the hogs were kept well-fed, and hens were continually setting. It was not unusual to have an abundance of well over one hundred ripe tomatoes to pick in one day. Apples, corn, wheat, and all were grown to feed both people and livestock. The farmers kept lean while the animals kept fat.

Cannot Warter the Horse

Nina to Delaware

"Hello grandmother how are you well I hope well the weather keeps cold and damp and cannot go out to get wood and warter the horse and I am the unhappyest little child you ever saw but aunt Susie lets me go with her to feed the chickens some times and pleases me I am coming up to see you soon as it gets warm weather you must come soon and rite soon from sugar baby Nina"

On average, horses should drink around 10 gallons of water per day. It is imperative to ensure that a horse stays well fed and watered, or else it is susceptible to disease. Maintaining a healthy and strong horse was almost as important as the health of a family member during the time when horses were the main source of transportation.

White Baby Roses

Sue to Ida

"Hello Ida how are you all by this time well I hope you sed you would like to board with me if I have any thing to eat I have bin cooking cabage but they have not got much head I think I can get peas by Tuesday I wish you could see the blue rose it is a dasy it is not as pretty as a oxeyedasy but the white baby rose is just as boutifull well I have no news you must come and stay a week soon as you can and tell your mother and Lillie they must come soon you write soon from Sue to Ida by by"

By the time of this letter, ox-eye daisies were a new addition to the United States. They had only been brought from Europe a few years prior. The wild flower can be used in salads, tea tonics, and as medicine for whooping cough and asthma.

Photo from landscapeofus.com

Killing the Big Hog
Nina to Delaware

"Hello grandmother how are you hope you have got well by this time we are all tolerable well we killed the big hog yesday and aunt dried up the lard out dooars to day and staid out most all day it is so warm if you are well enogh it looks like you could come to see us I am coming up there soon if I can you must come soon and rite soon by by from Nina"

After a pig has reached a weight greater than 240 pounds, it is known as a hog. The heaviest hog ever recorded was named Big Bill. He clocked in at a whopping 2,552 pounds.

Lard, particularly in the south, was used to make soap. It was also used in the same way that butter is used today in cooking, on bread, etc.

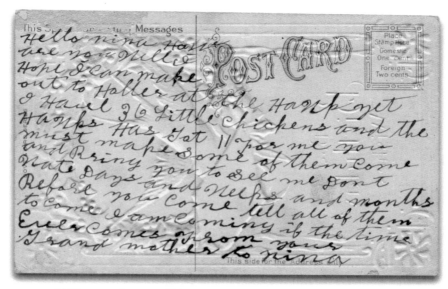

Hawks Got my Chickens
Delaware to Nina

"Hello Nina how are you well I hope I can make out to holler at the hawk yet I have 36 little chickens and the hawks has got 11 for me you must make some of them come and bring you to see me Dont wate days and weeks and months to come I am coming if the time ever comes from your Grand mother to Nina"

I can imagine Delaware, 70 years old, hobbling to her chicken coop with a broom while shouting mild vulgarity to swipe away any predators from her chickens.

This is a timeless struggle that is still relatable to chicken owners today. Coyotes, snakes, owls, hawks, and many other animals all provide constant threats to the well-being of the coop during day and night.

Delaware's Chickens

These little handmade chickens were most likely crafted by somebody in the family, probably one of Delaware's children. The main material feels like felted wool. The feet are wires wrapped in cardstock, the beak is also cardstock, the eyes are small black beads cut in half, and the wings are pieces of cotton fabric attached to the body in some way. Of course, there is a rooster to accompany the hen. I am unsure of the age, but it was in a box of other items dating from the turn of the century, pre-1910.

Sorry About your Chickens
Aubrey to Delaware

"Hello Grandmother how are you well I hope I am sorry to hear that the hawks catches your chickens they get some of Aunt Sues sometimes and Ninas too I could not go to town I did not have any shoes to wear but mama got me a pair of slippers and too new hats well grandmother you must come and write soon from Aubrey"

During this time, country mercantile stores carried everything that a farming family could possibly need. Country stores sold live hens, clothing, food, tools, and so on. Of course, the selection of clothing was not nearly as vast as the modern day, but people wore what they could get. Aubrey's hat was most likely priced around one dollar.

Picking Apples for Hogs
Delaware to Aubrey

"Hello Aubrey how are you you must come and stay a week with me and help me pick up apples for my hogs tell mother and aunt sue they must come and tell me something I cant go any where to hear any thing tell dadda not to kill his self at work you all must come real soon and write soon from grand mother"

In the first few months of a pig's life, before it reaches 250 pounds, it consumes around six to eight pounds of feed daily. The hogs that Delaware raised often grew to over 500 pounds. Of course, in order to reach that weight, the hog will have to consume much more than that weight in feed.

Old Whitmill Friends
Delaware to Sue

"Hello Sue how are getting on well I hope I am getting on veary well now I have bin to Whitmill this week I was veary glad to see my old friends one more time I am coming down on a spree to see you all before long I have sold 19 chickens and I have a yeard full left well my garden is veary common I have a veary nice lot of sweet potato slips ready for sitting out now well you must come real soon and rite soon from D G to Sue"

Whitmell was named in honor of state legislator Whitmell Pugh Tunstall (1810-1854) of Chatham. Before, it was known as Chestnut Grove. In 1878, Whitmell Farm-Life School was founded, which was the school my grandmother and mother attended. I'm unsure of what friends Delaware is referencing.

Whitmell School in 2015

A Hornet Sting
Nina to Delaware

"Hello grandmother how are you well I hope I am not so very well me and Aubrey has had bad colds and a hornet stung me to day and it did not feel good well I have bin atending the meeting at weal you aught to bin there well you must come soon as you can and rite soon so by by from Nina"

Hornets are the largest member of the wasp family and have the most painful sting. They're often found feeding on fallen fruit. They love to feed on the pear tree beside my house. Although, a hornet's favorite food is, in fact, bees (a hornet is not a bee, which is separate from the wasp family, although they are distantly related). Hornets only attack in self-defense, so I am sure this hornet put little Nina's day to misery.

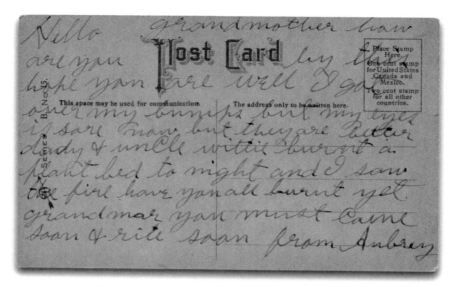

Burning Plant Beds
Aubrey to Delaware

"Hello grandmother how are you by this hope you are well I got over my bumps but my eyes is sore now but they are better dady & uncle willie burnt a plant bed to night and I saw the fire have you all burnt yet grandmar you must come soon & write soon from Aubrey"

Burning plant beds is just a way to get rid of the excess brush after the harvest is complete. For example, after the tomato plants have brought their full yield for the year, it was easier to put them in a big pile and have a bonfire rather than to haul them off somewhere to throw into the woods.

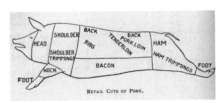

The handwritten postcard reads:

"Hello aubrey How are you Well I Hope you must Be a good little Boy and not cry you must come soon and see my two little Fat Piggs that I Got Last week tell Daddy and uncle Willie I would have Looked For one of them if it Had not Been Raining to Day Well you must come Joust as soon as you can and tell all the rest to come Write soon From your Grand mother"

Place Postage Stamp Here
Domestic One Cent
Foreign Two Cents

Little Fat Piggs

Delaware to Aubrey

"Hello Aubrey how are you well I hope you must be a good little boy and not cry you must come soon and see my two little fat piggs that I got last week tell daddy and uncle willie I would have looked for one of them if it had not been raining to day well you must come joust as soon as you can and tell all the rest to come write soon from your Grand mother"

Pigs could be purchased from neighboring farmers or at the market. It was tradition to raise pigs each year to kill by November.

See page **79** for more information on *hog killing*.

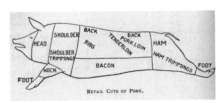

An illustration of retail cuts of pork from the book Farm Arithmetic by Charles William Burkett, 1916

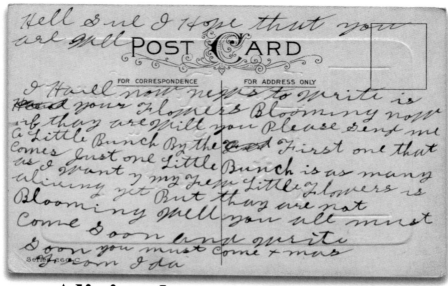

Aliving but not Blooming
Ida to Sue

"Hello Sue I hope that you are well I have now news to write is your flowers blooming now if thay are will you please send me a little bunch by the first one that comes just one little bunch is as many as I want my few little flowers is aliving yet but thay are not blooming well you all must come soon and write soon you must come xmas from Ida"

The women of the family loved their flowers. My great-grandmother, Louise Meadows Grant, often grew creeping flock alongside the road, which was her favorite. She also had lilac bushes and lilies sprouted around the yard. Her mother, Alice Pruett Meadows grew morning glories in an arch across the front porch (see page **10** for a photo).

Sow me some Seeds
Ida to Sue

"Hello Sue I am as fine as fiddle strings how are you by this time can you use your arm good now do it hurts you any now I hope not I wish I could see your pansies I know they are pretty you said did I have any pansies no I have not got any I am going to sow me some seeds you say you will send me some alright I wish you would send me ever flower that you have got ha ha I sure would thank you for them ha ha I want to get me a lot of flowers now for I have now got a good house to keep them in in the winter time harper said tell you all Hello you all must come and write real soon so with the best of wishes I will say good bye from Ida"

Sowing seeds has been the basis for many intellectual quotes about life. In the Holy Bible, 2 Corinthians says:

"The point is this: whoever sows sparingly will also reap sparingly, and whoever sows bountifully will also reap bountifully."

Grief Giles and Mrs. Powell
Ida to Mittie

"Hello Mit I am well and I hope this will find you all the same I am sorry to know that grief and his folks has been sick I hope thay are well by this time I am glad to know that mrs powell is well again I have no news worth telling I have one hen setting you all must come soon kiss the childern for me and bring them to see me soon come and write soon from Ida"

Grief Giles was a neighbor of John, Mittie, Willie, and Sue. He lived through the woods to the back of their home. I'm unsure of what sickness they had, but none of them died from it. Grief was born in 1870 and lived until 1937. Grief and Delaware were third cousins.

I believe the Mrs. Powell in this letter is Martha "Pattie" Parrish Powell (1864-1951), wife of William Elisha Powell, who is a cousin of mine through my grandfather who was a Powell. They lived next to Delaware.

39 Little Chickens
Ida to Sue

"Hello sue I am well and I hope this will find you the same well I have not got any good news to tell you only I have 39 little chickens and our garden is looking very well how is yours looking well you all must come soon I hope to get down thar agan some day write soon from Ida"

Chickens were generally saved to eat on special occasions. Of course, in Ida's time, chicken coops were not the norm. Chickens were free-range, which accounts for the high rate at which they get killed by predators. Chickens tend to lay anywhere between 80-150 eggs per year.

California Ranch Chickens, 1920
Photo from thehappychickencoop.com

The Companion
Ida to Sue

"Hello Sue I am well how are you I hope willies back has got well mamma said tell you hello and tell you to come and see her mamma is not well but she keeps up yes I planted snaps good Friday well I have sent for the companion for 12 months I told them to be sure to send the march number I have not got it yet I guess that it will come this week you can get it I wanted to be sure that I got that old mans ind haha you all must come and write soon from Ida"

In fact, Ida met her husband Harper through a segment of The Companion where one could have correspondence with men of interest.

The Companion, March 1912
Photo from Pinterest.com

A Funny Old Har
Aubrey to Delaware

"Hello grandmother how are you by this I hope you are well I am tobley well I have been with dady to get too lods of guano and mama went and got me a new suit and some slippers grandma this is not a pretty card but I think it is such a funny old har I want you to see it mama said we would run up there to see you soon as we can you must come soon & write soon from your little boy AJP"

"too lods of guano" refers to two loads of guano, which is what soil fertilizer was known as. Bird excrement (guano) is known as one of the world's best fertilizers due to its high nitrogen, phosphate, and potassium contents.

See page **152** to see the front of the card that Aubrey calls a funny old hare.

Dry of Whiskey
Ida to Sue

"Hello sue I am well and I hope you are the same well the state is dry I am glad of it but it will not be much better around here unless thay would kill ever body around here that knows how to make whiskey well you all must come and write soon from Ida well I have got to write to my husband to night bless his bones ha ha"

This seems to be one of the only cards written after 1915 since the state of Virginia became dry of alcohol in 1916 before the 19th amendment was enacted in 1920. Ida provided quite a realist opinion on the subject since she knew the ways of her neighbors, and she was right. Never did the country completely stop their production of alcohol, especially those who were involved with moonshine in the south.

The Plants is Up
Ida to Sue

"Hello sue how are you I am well and as fine as fiddle strings I am glad you can use your arm some hope it is well by this time my little flowers is looking fine you must bring me some more flowers when you come to see me harper said tell willie that his plants was up and was looking nice ha ha well you must make willie bring you to see us tell him if he dont bring you to see me that I am going to get mad and stick my mouth out ha ha come and write soon from Ida"

This letter is a continuation of the line of correspondence from page **124**.

Sue was around age 50 by the time of this letter, so injuries on the farm were expected. She may have fallen or pulled a muscle. Thankfully, it healed without any permanent damage.

Post Card

THIS SPACE FOR CORRESPONDENCE | THIS SPACE FOR ADDRESS ONLY

PLACE STAMP HERE.
UNITED STATES AND CANADA, ONE CENT.
FOREIGN TWO CENTS.

Chicks and Hens
Sue to Ida

"Hello Ida how are you by this we are all tolerable well and I hope you all the same well I have 7 little chicks and 5 hens setting how many have you all got we planted peas and onions yesterday have you planted yet I did not get the card you started if I had I would have written sooner well I have no news to rite tell your mother I will look for her the first warm Sunday and you must come and stay a week soon so by by from your friend Susie"

Since traveling was such a hassle without cars, family and friends tended to stay over quite a bit longer than a day or two. These letters often mention coming to stay a week. Most of us today could not stand staying a week with a relative, no matter how much we love them.

Delaware's Sun Bonnet

This sun bonnet is paired with the one on page **42**. This one does not cover the shoulders, though. The style looks to be circa 1890's as well.

CHAPTER SEVEN
Howdy to the Holidays

German traditions, Scandinavian celebrations, Pagan rituals, Dutch words, and English translations have been mixed, mashed, and twisted into the American celebration that everyone is familiar with today. Everyone's favorite Christmastime figure—Old St. Nicholas, Sinter Klaas, or Santy Claus—has been through many interpretations.

As the tradition goes, St. Nicholas tossed three golds coins down the chimney of a home that belonged to three peasant sisters, which landed in their stockings that were hung atop the hearth to dry out.

Although the first trees used by Germans to celebrate the Christmas season were oak, evergreen trees came soon after. The tradition was brought over by immigrants, but it was helped to spread across the rest of Europe and the Americas by Prince Albert (who was born in Germany) when he placed one at Windsor Castle in 1841.

Every major American holiday is tied together by the legends, cultures, traditions, and misconstrued natures of the world. It is hard to consider that holidays were ever any different than they are now, but most of what we celebrate annually has only reached its 'modern form' within the last century.

46 Star Flag -- Photo from etsy.com

The Prettiest Easter Rabet
Aubrey to Delaware

"Hello grandmother how are you well I hope I am taking me a good nap while mama rites this card to you dady maid me a whistle to day and I have the prettiest easter rabet that I ever saw aunt sue brought it from town well we are farming every day now you must come real soon & rite soon from Aubrey"

Receiving a pet rabbit for Easter is a tradition that still continues today, (for some) although most of the rabbits are given to the animal shelter. Nonetheless, during the time of Aubrey's childhood, it was magical.

The Prettiest Easter Chicken
Nina to Delaware

"Hello grandmother how are you well I hope I dont feel so well to day our lilacks are in bloom and they are so pretty I wish you would come now so you could see them dady made me a whistle to day and I have the prettiest easter chicken you ever saw mr whitehead sent it to me well you must come and rite soon from Nina"

Well, I guess Easter pets are not limited to rabbits. In fact, a chicken as an Easter pet seems like a much better option since rabbits do not lay Easter eggs. Mr. Whitehead probably refers to James Wyatt Whitehead Sr. of Chatham who ran the popular J.W. Whitehead & Son Store until his death in 1919.

J.W. Whitehead, ca. 1862

Expecting Xmas Presents
Delaware to Sue

"Hello Susin how are you by this time I hope you are well I dont feel so good to night tell willie hello for me tell mittie hello for me tell john hello for me I am expecting a xmas present from all four of you I have got three hens A laying how meny have you got well I will close for this time rite soon and come soon from DGP to SHP"

It seems that Delaware held a strict bargain. She did not simply wish for Christmas presents, they were *expected*. I sure hope her children and children-in-law didn't let her down. Perhaps she received another shipment of Lax-Fos for Christmas.

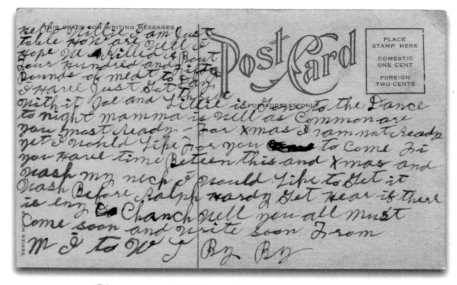

Come Wash my Neck
Ida to Willie

"Hello Willie I am just toble how are well I hope we killed a bout four hundred and fifty pounds of meat to day I have just got thrue with it Joe and Lillie is gone to the dance to night mamma is well as common are you most ready for xmas I am not ready yet I would like for you to come fi you have time beteen this and xmas and wash my neck I would like to get it wash before Ralph Hardy get hear if there is eny chanch well you all must come soon and write soon from M I to W T by by"

This is yet another example of Ida's peculiar behavior toward Ralph Hardy. I'm quite positive they went with each other for a short while. Also, I thought it was interesting that Ida wrote the word 'if' backwards, as "fi"

And yet of course Lillie and Joe have gone out dancing once again.

As (some versions of) the old song goes:
"How the heck can I wash my neck if it ain't a-gonna rain no mo'?"

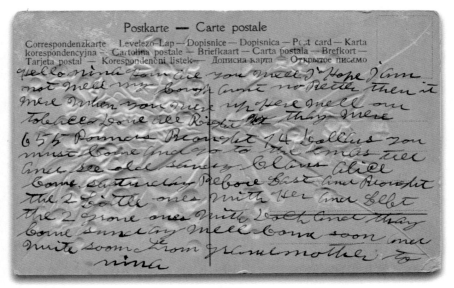

Postkarte — Carte postale

Correspondenzkarte — Levelező-Lap — Dopisnice — Dopisnica — Post card — Karta korespondencyjna — Cartolina postale — Briefkaart — Carta postala — Brefkort — Tarjeta postal — Korespondenčni listek — Дописна карта — Открытое письмо

Go to the Xmas Tree
Delaware to Nina

"Hello Nina how are you well I hope I am not well my cough aint no better then it were when you were up here well our tobacco done all right They were 655 pounds brought 74 dollars you must come and go to the xmas tree and see old sandy claus Alice come Saturday before last and brought the 2 little ones with her and left the 2 grone ones with Dock and thay come Sunday well come soon and write soon from grandmother to Nina"

$74 in this time is equivalent to about $1,907 in 2019.

The two little children of Dock and Alice refers to Oscar (b. 1908) and Louise Meadows (b. 1912), while the two grown children refer to Nettie (b. 1903) and Cassie Meadows (b. 1906).

My Jug Fill for Xmas

Joe to John

"Hello Jack how are you well I hope I am feeling all right I bin to the market this week mammas tobacco made 717 lb brought $63.00 well I havent much news only I getting ready to have my jug fill for x mas you must come up rite soon and come soon JEP to JBP by by tell my girl howdy and dont forget to shake hand with her"

Do you think Joe got his jug full of...eggnog? Christmas punch, perhaps? Whatever his jug was full of, I'm sure it was distilled right on the Dry Fork, Virginia countryside and it made his night a little happier.

This is only one of two letters I have that were written by Joe. I'm unsure why he didn't write much, although none of the men seemed to.

Just One Xmas Dance
Lillie to Mittie

"Hello Mittie how are you well I hope I am well how is the little ones getting one well I hope I sure did have a fine time xmas I never went to but one dance yes I sure was glad when that old man got married it tuched me mightly I want to come down there Saturday if Joe will come with me but if we dont come some of you all come Sunday and see us well I must stop for this time hoping to see you soon write soon and come soon from Lillie C Pruett to Mittie C Pruett"

Lillie only attended one dance? That is unheard of. Something must have been keeping her quite busy during the holiday. Although, I am glad to hear that she was still able to enjoy herself without having to attend at least one dance per night.

I'm unclear on which 'old man' she is referencing that got married.

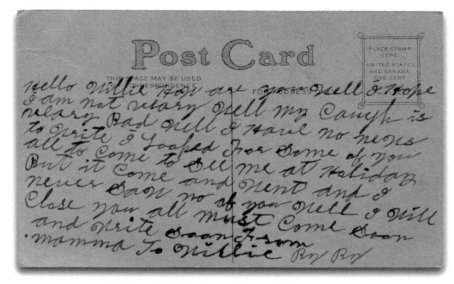

No Visit for Xmas
Delaware to Willie

"Hello willie how are you well I hope I am not veary well my cough is veary bad well I have no news to write I looked for some of you all to come to see me at holiday but it come and went and I never saw no of you well I close you all must come soon and write soon from mamma to willie by by"

This card made me sad. I'm sure that there was a reason that the family couldn't make it over to see their mother. Of course, it was all dependent on the horse instead of the automobile in this time.

Delaware's Box

I have kept this box organized in the same way it was the first time I ever opened it. Inside, sitting on a silk handkerchief, are two handmade chickens, (see page **116**) a beautiful broach which I have enhanced, and two small photos, one of Ida (page **174**) and Lillie (page **167**).

Lillie's Xmas Present
Lillie to Mittie

"Hello Mit how are you well I hope I am well say I hope you had a good time at xmas I did not have much of a time I did not go any where at all say did you get meny presents at xmas I got a nice bracelet for a xmas present it sure is nice you must come as soon as you can and tell willie I sed I would write and tell him the way to come up here if he did not know write soon and come soon from Lillie to Mittie"

Watches, pens, Kodak Brownie cameras, Victor Talking Machines, and jewelry were all extremely popular Christmas gifts during this time period. My grandmother still has a 1920 Victor Victrola that belonged to her grandmother, Alice Pruett Meadows.

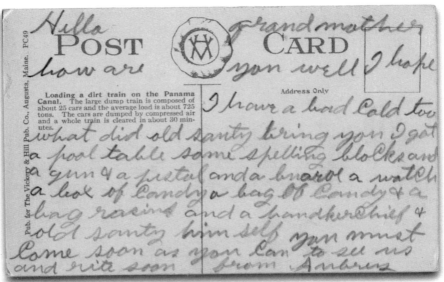

What did Old Santy Bring

Aubrey to Delaware

"Hello grandmother how are you well I hope what did old santy bring you I got a pool table some spelling blocks and a gun & a pistol and a buaroe a watch a box of candy a bag of candy & a bag rasins and a handkerchief & old santy him self you must come soon as you can to see us and rite soon from Aubrey"

Aubrey really racked up on this Christmas. a gun *and* a pistol, most likely a pellet rifle of sorts. The word 'buaroe' is a phonetic spelling of the word bureau, which is a desk. Aubrey will be eating candy 'til he's preserved.

A selection of old-fashioned hard candy - picture from candyattic.com

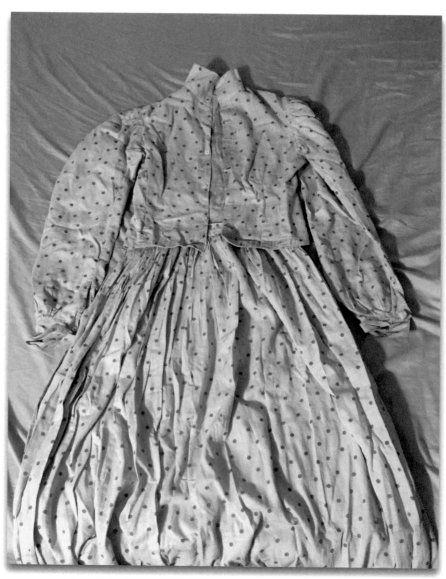

Delaware's dress soon after unboxing it for the first time, 2016

Delaware's Dress

My grandmother once told me the story of the old cedar chest. She'd come visit her grandmother's house, (Alice's house, where I live) go upstairs, and sift through the beautiful old clothing in the cedar chest. There was a dress she loved. It was cream colored with brown polka dots. Also in the chest were a few old bonnets. My grandmother loved to try on her great-grandmother's old clothing. The sun bonnets were a bit too big, so her aunt Nettie Meadows made her one to size.

We've never moved away from the property, so the dresses were surely still here somewhere, but where? We searched upstairs in my house, we searched closets at my grandmother's house, we searched more closets, I searched upstairs again, but I had no clue what it could be in. Then, in a little box that clothing comes in, there was a dress that looked like it was about to turn to dust. Thankfully, it cleaned up well, but it was dark green. I didn't know about a dark green dress, but there it was, in the box with two bonnets. I still wanted to find the one I was originally searching for, though; so, we searched and searched even more. Eventually, at the very top of the last closet we looked in, there was a box stuffed against the ceiling. It was relatively easy to get to, but it sure took long enough to discover it hiding there.

At last, it was the cream-colored dress. It was in pristine condition, and it instantly became my most prized possession. Like the bonnets that I have shown in previous pages (pp. **42** & **132**), both dresses seem to be from the 1890's. I believe both dresses are made of linen. The inside has quite a few self-repairs and hardworking stains from dreadful weather. The waist size of the skirt is extremely small, telling me that Delaware was a small framed woman. It fit my grandmother as a child relatively well, which also tells me that Delaware was not a tall woman either. See page **170** for a photo of my grandmother trying on the dress pictured at the left when she was a child. My hope is that this dress may keep forever in careful preservation, whether it is able to stay in the family or it is donated to a museum/historical society is for future generations to decide.

147 **Write Soon** | Kyle Griffith

Locks of Hair

When I was sifting through my box of family letters, documents, and heirlooms for the first time, I came across a folded-up piece of paper that had been tied tightly with a scrap of fabric. I thought it was going to be seeds, so I carefully loosened the knot and unraveled it with my hands cupped, though its contents were quite far from seeds. It was a large chunk of beautiful blonde hair. To me, a lock of hair is priceless. It is DNA, it is a piece of the person, and it is something that can never compare to a letter or item. Then I found three more.

Judging by the context of what else was in the box, the age of the paper the locks were folded in, and the nature of their color/ quantity, I have a good inference for who the hair belonged to. Following what I know about the children of Alice, the hair would go as follows: Nettie (blonde), Cassie (medium brunette), Oscar (strawberry blond and short hair), and Louise (dark brunette).

CHAPTER EIGHT
The Other Side

Of course, all of the post cards do have a backside; though, that is quite literally worth a whole book on its own. I have picked a selection that best represents the general collection of illustrations of the cards to display in this chapter. Most of the cards don't bare a sign of the company in which they were manufactured, but I've been able to research a few to find out more about them. The 'golden age' of postcards was, in fact, 1907-1915 due to the Universal Postal Congress allowing message space on the left half of the postcard's back.

The designs on the post card said a lot about the person writing it. Willie often used plain, unembellished cards, but he oftentimes didn't have much news to write. Ida sometimes ran out of her ordinary cards and had to tap into her stash of romantically themed cards.

Below is an envelope from the Columbus Card Company, which was a popular card manufacturer of the time. I believe it was included in the shipment of cards if the recipient desired to give feedback or had a complication with the company.

THIS LETTER IS FROM

Name _____

P. O. _____

State _____

Write R. F. D. No., Box No. or Street and No. on above line.
PLEASE FILL IN THE ABOVE

Be sure and put on a two-cent stamp here, and see that your letter is properly sealed.

Columbus Card Co.
Columbus, Ohio.

Many of the cards are themed around the holidays. Above is one for Valentine's Day, and below is one for Easter.

(**Above**) Lillie often signed her cards on the back using colorful glitter ink. She was the type to bedazzle and customize anything she put her hands on.

(Above) This card was remarked by Aubrey Pruett to be "such a funny old har."

(Above) *"Say nothing, saw wood"* is an old saying which means to refrain from saying anything that might stir drama. In other words: *bite your tongue.*

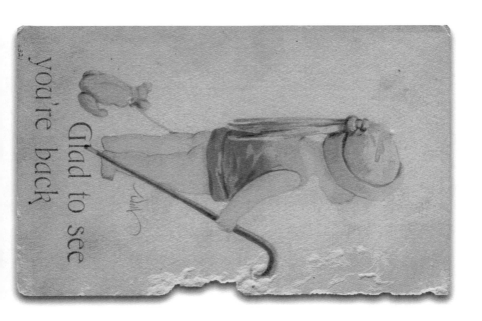

(**Above**) This one took me off guard when I found it. It is a 1912 dutch boy postcard illustrated by Bernhardt Wall, an extremely well-known illustrator and historian.

Oftentimes Ida ran out of neutral-themed cards and had to delve into her supply of romantic cards that she saved for men of potential interest.

Below is a personal favorite design of mine.
I'm the man to marry for I can make the "dough"

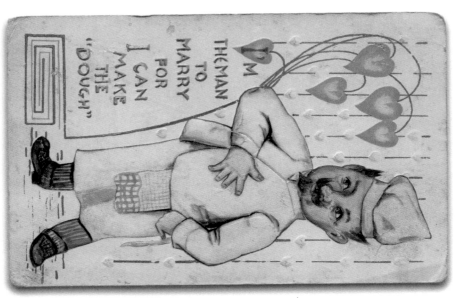

The above card offers a humorous yet true piece of poetry: *Man's love is like scotch snuff—you take a pinch and that's enough. Profit by this sage advice, when you fall in love, think twice.*

Below is an interesting card with macabre humor. It is the first variation in the "Bad Dream Series" of postal cards, possibly a theme intended for the Halloween season.

I DREAMT I was in a trance, my folks thought me dead. They put me in a coffin; they cried and said nice things about me. All night long the old cat whose kittens I had drowned that morning, sat on my coffin and gloated over my sufferings, she knew I was alive. I was placed in a hearse and in due time arrived at the grave yard. I could hear the mud hit the lid of the coffin and began to choke when I woke up

Above shows the reverse side's additional writing which is a continuation of the card "Hevening Company" featured on page **92**.

PAID IN FULL

159 **Write Soon** | Kyle Griffith

Above is another favorite of mine—a simple, yet clever play on words sure to put a smile on its intended recipient.
A pair of suspenders

THE GALLERY

Believe it or not, all of the names in this book have a face to go with them; although, some had their photo taken and others did not. Through some extremely convoluted and tenacious nature, I have ended up with most all of the family photos.

To my despair, Ephraim Pruett and his wife Delaware did not agree with the practice of having one's photograph taken, so they are forever faceless—unless you have got the determination and inability to accept such a blasphemous concept such as I. Of course, I have developed a rendered a conceptual piece of what I believe Ephraim and Delaware to have looked like. Using key facial features from their sons, I have merged together a general likeness for Ephraim. Using facial features from the daughters as well as eyes from Delaware's brother, Scott, I have devised a potential likeness for her as well. That picture is shown below. I placed the faces on (edited) bodies from an 1860's portrait.

(Above) Circa 1911; Permelia Alice Pruett (1881-1960) with her husband Dock Franklin Meadows and their first three children which are as follows: (left to right) Nettie Green Meadows, Oscar Franklin Meadows, and Cassie E. Meadows.

(Left) Alice bearing her head full of snow-white hair as all of her grandchildren remember her.

(Above) Ruth Ellen Pruett (1877-1959) most likely wrote letters, but I don't believe that any have survived the passage of time. She is only mentioned once in all of the correspondence when she has lost her baby. Ruth married a blacksmith named Joseph Harris "Joe" Lynch. He ran his shop at the end of my driveway on Dry Fork Road in a long wooden building that still stands to this day. The building was later used as a house by a child of Cassie Meadows named Aurelian Shelton, though he was better known by his nickname "Sheriff." Ruth and Joe had four children who lived to adulthood: Reuben James, Joseph Ravion, Monroe Suthern, and Effie May Lynch.

(Above) Rebecca Louise "Becky" Pruett and her husband Robert Hobson Meadows. Becky is not known to have written letters, but I have one by her daughter Lottie. The children from left to right are as follows: Robert Green "Bobby," Minnie, and Lottie Meadows

(Left) Nina Evalena Pruett Edmunds (1909-2000) holds a vase of flowers. Her face is reminiscent of her mother's. She was the last living person to have first-hand knowledge of the memories expressed throughout this book. She married Coleman Bennett Edmunds and had one child, Mittie Lou Edmunds. Nina was a Pittsylvania County school teacher for many years.

(Above) Circa 1905; Permelia Alice Pruett (1881-1960) and her husband Dock Franklin Meadows with their first child, Nettie Green Meadows, who was born the day the Old 97 wrecked in Danville, Virginia (September 27, 1903).

(Left) Circa 1945; Alice stands with one of her sons Harry Clay Meadows Sr. in front of their home one last time before moving to their newly built home up the road in Dry Fork.

(Above) Sidney Jackson "Sid" Pruett (1867-1929) never wrote letters from what I can tell. He is not mentioned in any of the correspondence and not much is known of him. He married a woman from Callands named Mintola Collins but had no children. He must have been liked, though, since I have a 20 inch tall portrait of him in my possession that belonged to his sister Alice. **(Below)** Mary Ida Pruett (1886-1980) in her old age; mid 1960's

(Right) Lillie Carr Pruett (1889-1957) eventually took enough of a break from dancing in order to marry James Edward "Jim" Jones. Together, they had six children. The first two born, Mildred and Jim Jr., are pictured here. Directly below is another photo of Lillie years before.

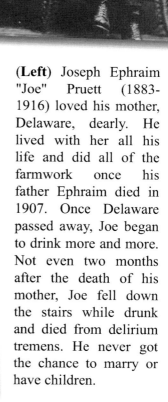

(Left) Joseph Ephraim "Joe" Pruett (1883-1916) loved his mother, Delaware, dearly. He lived with her all his life and did all of the farmwork once his father Ephraim died in 1907. Once Delaware passed away, Joe began to drink more and more. Not even two months after the death of his mother, Joe fell down the stairs while drunk and died from delirium tremens. He never got the chance to marry or have children.

William Thomas "Willie" Pruett (1868-1945) and his wife Susan Harris "Sue" Watson Pruett were happily married, although they never had children. Willie developed cancer in his right arm, which led to his death in 1945.

**Mittie Cora
Watson Pruett**
(1875-1946)

(Above) Christmas day, 1941. Left to right show Willie, Aubrey, Nina & Dog "Petie," Mittie, and John Ballard Pruett.
(Below) 1962, my grandmother, Margaret Grant, is sporting the dress and bonnet of her great-grandmother, Delaware Watson Pruett.

Aubrey Jackson
Pruett
(1910-1966)

Nina Evalena Pruett Edmunds (1909-2000)

(Right) Mittie Cora Watson Pruett (1875-1946) holds her only granddaughter of the same name, Mittie Lou Edmunds. Baby Mittie was born in 1945 and her grandmother passed away the following year. This book would not be possible without the contributions by young Mittie pictured here, and I am honored to still know her well.

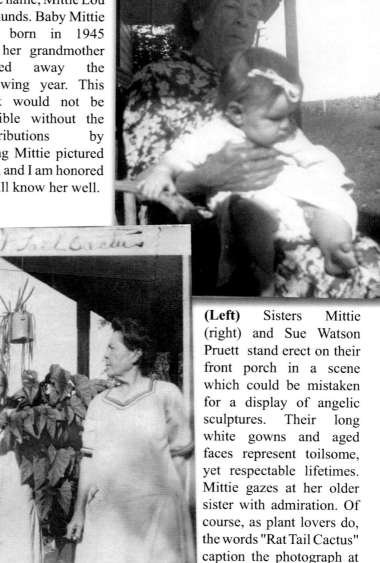

(Left) Sisters Mittie (right) and Sue Watson Pruett stand erect on their front porch in a scene which could be mistaken for a display of angelic sculptures. Their long white gowns and aged faces represent toilsome, yet respectable lifetimes. Mittie gazes at her older sister with admiration. Of course, as plant lovers do, the words "Rat Tail Cactus" caption the photograph at the top to educate viewers on the contents of the hanging pot.

Mary Ida Pruett
Kernodle Pyle
(1886-1980)

(Left) John Ballard Pruett (1873-1960) poses for quite an impressive portrait around the turn of the century. One would never think that he was actually a farmer who wore overalls and got his hands dirty (see page **57**). He was a family man who worked hard to earn his true living. He kept a fine mustache his whole life.

(Right) George Scott Watson (1859-1922) was the brother of Delaware Watson Pruett. Scott never married, although he did have an illegitimate son with a young lady named Donnie Odelle Emerson (1874-1953). The son took his mother's last name and his father's first; he was George Henry Emerson (1890-1974). George, in fact, married Minnie Bell Meadows, daughter of Robert H. Meadows and Becky Pruett (page **164**). George and Minnie had around nine children, one of which, Alfred Emerson, served as the Postmaster to Dry Fork.

REFERENCES

Access, Ray. "Appalachian Hog-Killing Tradition." *Simply Appalachian*, 30 Oct. 2015, www.simplyappalachian.com/article/2015/10/appalachian-hog-killing-tradition.

Bickers, Chris. "Virginia Tobacco Growers Battled through Hardest Growing Season." *Farm Progress*, Informa Markets, 3 Dec. 2016, www.farmprogress.com/tobacco/virginia-tobacco-growers-battled-through-hardest-growing-season.

Blakemore, Erin. "Poorhouses Were Designed to Punish People for Their Poverty." *History*, A&E Television Networks, 30 Jan. 2018, www.history.com/news/in-the-19th-century-the-last-place-you-wanted-to-go-was-the-poorhouse.

Book, Ethan. "From Pig to Pork Chop: the Rising Costs Of Raising Food." *Epicurious*, Conde Nast, 28 Aug. 2008, www.epicurious.com/archive/blogs/editor/2008/08/from-pig-to-por.html.

Byron, Morgan A., and Jennifer L. Gillett-Kaufman. "Tobacco Hornworm." *Entomology and Nematology Department*, University of Florida, Oct. 2017, entnemdept.ufl.edu/creatures/field/tobacco_hornworm.htm.

Christian, Brad. "What Is Flue Cured Tobacco?" *Whole Leaf Tobacco Blog,* Total Leaf Supply, 20 Nov. 2018, totalleafsupply.com/what-is-flue-cured-tobacco/.

Driver, Pearl. "3 Signs of a Sweet and Juicy, Ready to Eat Peach." *Frog Hollow Farm*, 21 May 2014, www.froghollow.com/blogs/news/14211125-3-signs-of-a-sweet-and-juicy-ready-to-eat-peach.

"Farm Wife, 1900." *EyeWitness to History*, Ibis Communications, 2007, www.eyewitnesstohistory.com/farmwife.htm.

Gilliam, Steve. "Tobacco: Brought Danville, Virginia, Fame and Fortune." *NCCCHA*, Caswell County Historical Association, 4 July 2010, ncccha.blogspot.com/2010/07/tobacco-brought-danville-virginia-fame.html.

Happy Chicken Coop. "A History of Chickens: Then (1900) Vs Now (2016)." *The Happy Chicken Coop*, 1 Oct. 2015, www. thehappychickencoop.com/a-history-of-chickens/.

Hill, H. J. "The History of Brush Arbors." *The Classroom*, 17 May 2019, www.theclassroom.com/the-history-of-brush-arbors-12080347.html.

"Hornet Facts." *SoftSchools*, www.softschools.com/facts/animals/ hornet_facts/1404/.

Johnson, Sarah. "A Guide to Southern Accents and Sayings." *WanderWisdom*, HubPages Inc, 12 Oct. 2018, wanderwisdom. com/travel-destinations/A-Guide-to-Southern-Accents.

"Just How Did We Get That Tradition?" North Platte Nebraska's Newspaper, 22 Dec. 2007, www.nptelegraph.com/just-how-did-we-get-that-tradition/article_8f18a109-93d0-579c-9b35-50adc2f1add5.html?mode=jqm.

Lively, Joe. *Notes of a Time Traveler: Our Forgotten Folk Heritage.* Amelia Bulletin Monitor, 2000.

McKinley, Don. "The Right Tool for the Job: Husking Corn by Hand - Equipment." *Farm Collector*, Ogden Publications, Inc., Nov. 2015, www.farmcollector.com/equipment/tools/husking-corn-by-hand-zm0z15novzhur.

Montgomery, Michael. "Hain't We Got a Right to Use Ain't and Auxiliary Contraction?: Toward a History of Negation Variants in Appalachian English." *Artsandsciences*, Southern Journal of Linguistics, 2014, artsandsciences.sc.edu/appalachianenglish/ sites/default/files/Montgomery 2014 - Hain't we got a right to use ain't and auxiliary contraction_.pdf.

Naughton, Jim. "The Last Poorhouse in Virginia." *The Washington Post*, WP Company, 18 July 1990, www.washingtonpost.com/archive/ lifestyle/1990/07/18/the-last-poorhouse-in-virginia/106eca8b-1569-4f9e-8ff3-74d7d7c5166a/?noredirect=on&utm_term=. a765c6a22a1b.

Old and Interesting. "Butter-Making - Home Churns and Utensils." *Butter Churns - History of Domestic Butter-Making*, www. oldandinteresting.com/history-butter-churns.aspx.

"Postcard History." *Smithsonian Institution Archives*, 19 Sept. 2013, siarchives.si.edu/history/featured-topics/postcard/postcard-history.

Propst, Sarah. "High Mountains, Flatfeet: The History of Clogging in Appalachia." *Medium*, Spring 2018 Introduction to Appalachian Studies Research, 9 May 2018, medium.com/spring-2018-introduction-to-appalachian-studies/high-mountains-flatfeet-the-history-of-clogging-in-appalachia-360c78ec4f5d.

Sabatella, Matthew. "A Brief History of Southern Square Dance." *American Heritage Music*, 21 Dec. 2018, www. americanheritagemusic.com/square-dance/.

The Museum of Yesterday. "Life in the Mid-20th Century American Home." *Home Life in The 20th Century*, www.demajo.net/20th_cent_home/index.htm.

Thompson, Derek. "Long Hours, Crowded Houses, Death by Trolley: America in 1915." *The Atlantic*, Atlantic Media Company, 11 Feb. 2016, www.theatlantic.com/business/archive/2016/02/america-in-1915/462360/.

Wallace, Eric J. "Bright Leaf Legacy." *Virginia Living*, 7 Nov. 2018, www.virginialiving.com/culture/bright-leaf-legacy/.

Wikipedia Contributors. "Whitmell P. Tunstall." *Wikipedia,* Wikipedia, the Free Encyclopedia, 24 Sept. 2018, en.wikipedia.org/wiki/Whitmell_P._Tunstall.

Yeatts, S. Dail. *Along the Dry Fork Road - Revised Edition*. Yeatts, 2016.

Ziegler, Michelle. "The Spotty History of Chicken Pox." *Contagions*, Wordpress, 27 May 2014, contagions.wordpress.com/2014/05/27/the-spotty-history-of-chicken-pox/.

In memory of my great-great grandparents, Dock Meadows and Alice Pruett Meadows, who serve as the gateway for me to behold the beautiful memories they developed. It is my wish that Alice may forever live vicariously through the preservation of her letters and heirlooms to archive her priceless knowledge so future generations can learn from my family's lives.

My drawing of Dock Franklin Meadows (1882-1942) and his wife, Permelia Alice Pruett Meadows (1881-1960). Pencil on 110lb cardstock, 8x10in, 2019.

ABOUT THE AUTHOR

Kyle Griffith practices genealogy, graphic design, pencil portraiture, and 18th century living history. Pittsylvania County and his native community of Dry Fork, Virginia are the sources of much of his inspiration. He has won regionally in the Young Authors program three times. Since 2016, Kyle has been active in many local organizations including the Pittsylvania County Historical Society, where he writes articles for quarterly publications; Chatham First, where he serves as Co-Chairman of the Calendar Committee in designing the annual calendar; and multiple fraternal groups. "Write Soon" is his first full-length title; his goal is to preserve and make sure that history lives longer than he does. Reach Kyle through his email—
kyleg434@gmail.com.